The Art & Craft of
COFFEE COCKTAILS

The Art & Craft of
COFFEE COCKTAILS

Over 75 recipes for mixing coffee and liquor

JASON CLARK

With photography by Alex Attikov Osyka

RYLAND PETERS & SMALL
LONDON • NEW YORK

Designer Paul Stradling
Editor Dawn Bates
Production David Hearn
Picture research Christina Borsi
Art Director Leslie Harrington
Editorial Director Julia Charles
Publisher Cindy Richards

Indexer Hilary Bird

Published in 2018 by
Ryland Peters & Small
20–21 Jockey's Fields
London WC1R 4BW
and
341 E 116th St
New York NY 10029

www.rylandpeters.com

Text and commissioned photography
© Jason Clark 2018

For full picture credits, see right

ISBN: 978-1-78879-043-7

A CIP record for this book is available
from the British Library.
US Library of Congress Cataloging-in-
Publication data has been applied for.

10 9 8 7 6 5 4 3 2 1

Printed and bound in China

*This book is dedicated to my No.1 supporter, friend and
favourite cocktail-loving customer, Girl Sam Gilmore.
I have no doubt she would have made her way through
every single recipe in this book were she still sitting at
my bar. This one's for you Sam.*

Notes

• Both British (metric) and American (Imperial ounces plus
US cups) measurements are included in these recipes for your
convenience; however, it is important to work with one set of
measurements only and not alternate between the two
within a recipe.

• All spoon measurements are level unless otherwise specified.

Picture credits

Photographs by Alex Attikov Osyka, except for:
14 Joy Skipper/Getty Images
16l Dirk Funhoff/Getty Images
16r Fine Art Images/Heritage Images/Getty Images
17 ©Hulton-Deutsch Collection/CORBIS/Corbis via Getty Images
18r De Agostini/Biblioteca Ambrosiana/Getty Images
19 GABRIEL BOUYS/AFP/Getty Images
20 Somsak Khamkula/EyeEm/Getty Images
21 John Coletti/Getty Images
22 Aaron McCoy/Getty Images
23l Jason Bakker/EyeEm/Getty Images
23r Diego Lezama/Getty Images
24 andresr/Getty Images
25l George Peters/Getty Images
25r Prashanth Vishwanathan/Bloomberg/Getty Images
26l Michael Marquand/Getty Images
26r Mint Images/Tim Pannell/Getty Images
27l Adam Gault/Getty Images
27r Michael Marquand/Getty Images
32 Westend61/Getty Images
33 Library of Congress - edited version © Science Faction/
Getty Images
34l Adam Gault/Getty Images
48 Nathan ALLIARD/Getty Images

CONTENTS

FOREWORD

Martin Hudak
The American Bar at the Savoy Hotel London
World Coffee in Good Spirits Champion 2017

The Art & Craft of Coffee Cocktails is a publication that has been missing in our industry for many years. This fantastic combination of two different fields showcases easy-to-use recipes complemented with delicious pictures. It is a must-have for all drinks lovers and industry professionals. May you enjoy many a coffee cocktail while reading this inspirational book!

Cheers,
Martin

Gary Regan
Legendary bartender and author of numerous bar industry titles such as
The Joy of Mixology, *The Negroni*, *The Bartenders' Gin Compendium* and more

When Jason Clark speaks, bartenders listen. It's a sure sign that, when it comes to cocktails, he has a firm grasp on what's going on behind the bars of the world. And to prove it, he's first out of the gate with a book about the hottest drinks trend in the world: coffee cocktails. The Espresso Martini, created by the late, great bartending legend, Dick Bradsell, was, I believe, the drink that started all the fuss, and if you've ever tasted one of these babies, you'll know what all the fuss is about. But Jason takes the whole concept of all coffee cocktails to a new level by examining every aspect of each drink within these pages. Here you'll learn about different styles of coffee, how to make them, and you'll discover why Jason chooses specific varieties for each drink that appears in his book. Indeed, there's a good chance that you'll emerge from this book as a fully qualified coffee geek. Wouldn't that be a treat?! And your adventure through this tome will be a very entertaining trip, indeed, as Jason takes you by the hand and imparts his wisdom in his own unique style. You'll be mentored, and you won't even realize it's happening.

Gary

INTRODUCTION

It is my utmost pleasure to introduce this collection of recipes, created over the course of 20-plus years working in the drinks industry. It is designed to educate, motivate and inspire readers of all levels, from beginners to already experienced bartenders and baristas, into combining two of life's greatest pleasures – coffee and liquor – in creative and, most importantly, delicious ways!

Both the coffee and cocktail industries are currently revelling in golden eras of quality and creativity, something that can be almost entirely put down to the professional, passionate and creative bartenders and baristas found in arguably every city in the world, working long hours towards the development and progression of their chosen crafts.

More often than not, however, these two kindred trades are kept worlds apart; coffee rules the light and liquor the night.

These often unsung heroes of our morning meetings and 5 'o'clock Fridays continue to raise the bar to lofty new heights day in, day out, striving for that perfect serve – not only to put bums on seats and bucks in the bank, but also to put smiles on the faces of an endless stream of nameless strangers in search of a little extra joy in their day.

For both bartenders and baristas, ticking all of these boxes brings an often unspoken sense of fulfilment, one that's hard to find in the countless other potential careers that are shunned in favour of a dirty apron, tired feet, cracked fingers and the unsociable hours found on the stage that is the bar or the counter.

I fell for the bar first and the bean second. Being a night owl, I've generally managed to avoid early mornings almost as much as I avoid instant coffee, but a motivational caffeine pep-talk quickly became a part of my daily bar routine as I looked for ways to retain energy and keep a smile on my face into the wee hours of the morning. As coffee and cocktails both played such important roles in my life, mixing the two together just seemed natural.

Today there is one coffee cocktail that rules them all – the Espresso Martini. This classic cocktail has hit an all-time high in popularity, with guests all around the world ordering it in record numbers. Espresso machines have also slowly but surely become an almost compulsory piece of bar apparatus and, with this addition, bartenders are expected to be able to shake up the unmistakably delicious, boozy, bitter-sweet velvet we have come to know and love so well until all hours of the night, leaving bartenders hating the 3 a.m. coffee-machine clean down at the end of service.

I'll delve deeper into the phenomenon that is the Espresso Martini later in the book, as well as introduce you to plenty of other examples of combining the qualities of coffee and liquor to make delicious and invigorating cocktails for the drinking pleasure of your friends, guests and, just as importantly, yourself.

But first let's look at how combining coffee with liquor adds the essential elements of both flavour and mouthfeel to your cocktails:

FLAVOUR Coffee has a strong and distinctive flavour most people tend to either love or hate. Every brew is made up of dozens of flavour nuances. If we take a typical cup of coffee and break it down to identify the taste, people will generally sound out cacao, toffee, toasted spices and nuts. This means it will naturally pair with other ingredients that have similar flavours. Examples include, but aren't limited to, aged rum and tequila, brandy, amaro, whiskies from Ireland, Scotland, America and everywhere in between, along with so many more spirits and liqueurs, and we therefore know that we can very easily pair them with coffee.

Besides all of these obvious flavours there are plenty of less obvious ones coffee can be paired to work well with (depending on the brew), such as beetroot, grapefruit, berries, apple, orange, passionfruit, stone fruits and so many more.

Coffee can be used either as a base flavour for the drink, dominating all the other flavours it's matched to like in an Espresso Martini or Irish Coffee, or less commonly it can be used as a modifier flavour. A small amount is added to play a supporting role to the other flavours in the drink. For example, adding a dash or two of coffee bitters to an Old Fashioned for a subtle influence.

MOUTHFEEL Along with flavour and aroma, coffee can also add a tremendous amount of mouthfeel to a cocktail. We tend to think of bitter and/or sweet or even sour characters. Mouthfeel can also be light, heavy, fluffy, cold, warm or hot depending on how the coffee is extracted. These are all elements you should consider when making or ordering a coffee cocktail.

I hope that this book will help to educate, inspire and, most importantly, whet your appetite to mix and drink these often-maligned man-made liquids of magnificence.

Enjoy!

Drinks Geek
Jason Clark

USING THIS BOOK

I assume that if you've read this far you already have an interest in both making and drinking coffee and cocktails… well, high five to that! In the following pages, I aim to give you a deeper understanding of both and share a few tips and tricks for mixing coffee cocktails, as well as making other useful ingredients and products such as bitters, liqueurs and foams.

KIT Having the right tools can help a lot when it comes to constructing fancy cocktails, so take a look at pages 12–15 to see what I recommend. But, remember, all this kit is not always necessary. Feel free to improvise any way you can – for example, jam jars make good shakers and rolling pins make great muddlers. It's all about doing the best you can with what you've got available.

Preparation is the key: I recommend selecting the recipes you want to make and laying out your tools and ingredients neatly first to make sure you have everything you need, and to make the overall process easier on yourself. Clean as you go and place items back in the same place immediately after use to help you to work faster and more efficiently with clarity

COFFEE The section on coffee (see pages 16–31) is designed to give curious readers a beginner- to intermediate-level insight into the history, cultivation, harvest and production of good-quality coffee, to build appreciation of this very special part of our day-to-day lives. Following this, on pages 32–49, I look into a variety of different brewing techniques, including instructions and tips on how to make great coffee. I recommend using this section to help you learn how to brew good coffee to drink on its own and/or to use in cocktails.

If you're already a pro, I hope you can pick up a few tricks to add to your repertoire as you flick through the chapters. For those with less experience, join me on a step-by-step journey through the next few pages to build yourself a great platform to develop your passion further and advance your abilities for mixing or ordering coffee cocktails.

TYPE OF COCKTAIL The recipes are organized into chapters based on how they are made – shaken, hot, built, stirred or thrown, and blended – so select the style of drink you want and proceed from there.

INGREDIENTS Homemade ingredients will either be detailed on the page or given a page reference to a longer, more complex recipe elsewhere in the book.

NOTES Certain liquor elements may not be available in your area and, as coffee is hugely dependent on how it's made and with what, I have added Coffee and Liquor notes to each recipe. These give recommendations and often alternative suggestions to help you flex them to suit your personal needs.

PHOTOS There's a photo of every cocktail to give you a clear indication of how the finished product should look, but feel free to use whatever glassware you have at hand and

finish the drinks your own way. Bartending is all about evolving and innovating recipes, so be creative!

SKILL LEVEL Each recipe comes with a difficulty rating (see right). At the start of each chapter, there is a simple classic recipe that has proven over time to be an iconic serve. From there on the difficulty slowly increases, so depending on your experience, skill level and access to advanced equipment, you can start easy and work your way up, or just jump in at the deep end. I hope the more challenging recipes will inspire you to both mix and order more interesting coffee

cocktails at home and in bars and cafes around the world. Look for these skill rating icons at the start of each recipe:

Beginner
Fairly simple drinks that only require basic tools – start with these if you are a novice.

Intermediate
More advanced drinks that may require more specialist ingredients and techniques.

Expert
Complex cocktails that require specialist items and are more suited to experienced bartenders.

USEFUL KIT

Both bartenders and baristas use a specific sets of tools to achieve high-quality drinks. Stunning precision tools, hand-crafted by Japanese samurais and German nuclear physicists, are becoming more and more readily available both online and in kitchen and hospitality stores. Though nice to have, these items are not essential, particularly when mixing drinks at home. A little bit of ingenuity goes a long way, so improvise and make do with what you have.

In these pages I've detailed the main items you will need, along with a few suggestions for more commonly available alternatives. The photographs show an extensive selection of the items professionals should have in their toolbox. If you want to buy any of the top tools, or perhaps just drool over all the shiny bling, go to www.muddle-me.com where you will find an incredible selection of everything you may want and more, all of which can be ordered online and shipped internationally.

Cocktails

COCKTAIL SHAKER A two-piece Boston shaker is the shaker of preference for most bartenders due to its ease of use. Alternatively, use a three-piece cobbler shaker, or even a large, solid glass jar will do.

JIGGER A device for measuring small quantities of liquid is essential. A shot glass, egg cup or baking measurement spoons will do if you don't have a bar-specific tool.

HAWTHORNE STRAINER Designed to fit on to the mouth of a shaker to quickly separate liquids, for example from ice and fruit pulp, this is an essential piece of bar kit. Alternatively, a large slotted kitchen spoon can work too.

BARSPOON Professional barspoons have multiple uses and are extremely useful. They are predominantly used for stirring and swizzling drinks. For this purpose, one with a long, spiralled handle is best; otherwise improvise with a tablespoon or wooden spoon. Barspoons are also used for measuring out small (5 ml) quantities so as a substitute a 5 ml measuring spoon could also be used.

ICE SCOOP This often-forgotten tool is essential for both speed and hygiene as it transfers the ice to your shaker or glass with ease, whilst keeping grubby paws from contaminating the drink. A sturdy coffee mug works well as a substitute. Never scoop ice with glass as it may chip and you may end up with glass in your drink.

GLASSWARE The glass you choose makes a huge difference to the look, feel and overall appreciation of your completed drink, so a mixed selection of fine-quality glassware (as seen throughout this book) is naturally preferred. However, don't be afraid to improvise and make do with what you have. Some of the best drinks I've ever had have been served in glasses from a thrift shop, jam jars or even disposable coffee cups

Top row: Jigger; Peeler; Hawthorne strainer; Strainer; Sieve; Strainer

Centre (clockwise): Mini-grater, Tongs, Muddler, Swizzle stick, Barspoon, Knife

Bottom row: Cocktail shaker, Mixing glass, Dasher, Atomizer, Cocktail sticks, Ice scoop

Coffee

DIGITAL SCALES Nowadays, even water is often weighed so digital scales are essential to help you with both accuracy and consistency in your brewing.

BURR GRINDER Accurately ground coffee is the key to getting the most out of your beans. Luckily quality grinders are now available at much more affordable prices than even a few years back. Look for one that's easily adjustable and hard-wearing.

GOOSENECK KETTLE Designed for accurate pouring, these quality kettles also come with digital controls for reaching and holding accurate temperatures.

STAINLESS STEEL MILK JUG Ideal for heating, aerating and pouring milk accurately.

TODDY COLD BREW HOPPER I am a huge fan of the Toddy Cold Brew extraction system (see page 41). It's so easy to make large batches of consistently great coffee with a 2–3 week shelf life.

Other useful tools

- Apron
- Atomizer bottle
- Bitters dasher
- Chopping board
- Cinnamon duster
- Filter paper
- Julep strainer
- Measuring jug/pitcher
- Measuring spoon
- Mini spice grater
- Mixing glass
- Paintbrush (for clearing loose coffee grinds)
- Peeler for zesting
- Sharp knife
- Small basket strainer
- Superbags
- Muddler/rolling pin
- Tea towels/dish towels
- Tongs
- Vacuum seal bags

Above: A good-quality household electric burr grinder.

Top row: Chemex jar; Plastic jug/pitcher; Stovetop moka pot; Measuring spoon; Drip brew system

Middle row: Copper kettle; Filter papers

Bottom row: French Press (cafetière); Burr grinder; Ground coffee jar; Digital scales

COFFEE TIMELINE

A fascinating look at coffee through the ages.

An Ethiopian goat herder notices his goats are overly energetic from eating cherries. He takes these cherries to a local monastery; the monks realize that chewing the cherries allows them to stay up late and achieve more work.

Iranian physician Avicenna describes the medicinal benefits of coffee as "A digestive and vascular system aid."

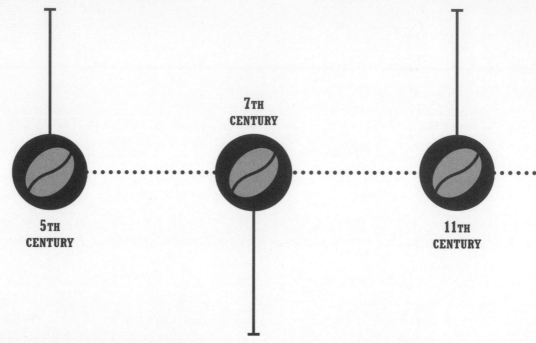

7TH CENTURY

5TH CENTURY

11TH CENTURY

Muslim pilgrims bring coffee to Yemen. Here they discover that roasting and brewing the beans makes an energizing tea. They begin to cultivate coffee trees in the mountains called Qahwa – the Arabic word for coffee.

- European travellers visit the Middle East and discover coffee. It soon starts to spread back home...
- **1647:** Venice opens its first coffee house, *Bottega Del Cafe.*
- **1650:** England opens its first coffee house, *Penny University, Oxford.*
- **1652:** London opens its first coffee house, *Virginia Coffee House.*
- **1673:** Germany opens its first coffee house, *Schutting.*
- **1675:** King Charles II bans coffee shops because he thinks that people are meeting there to conspire against him.
- **1677:** Hamburg opens its first coffee house.
- **1683:** Vienna opens its first coffee house; the creation of the Melange.
- **1685:** The Dutch begin to grow coffee in their colonies.
- **1688:** A coffee house, *Edward Lloyds* (see picture, right) opens in London. It later develops into the world's largest insurance company.
- **1689:** Paris opens its first coffee house, *Cafe Procope.*
- **1696:** New York opens its first coffee house, *The King's Arms.*

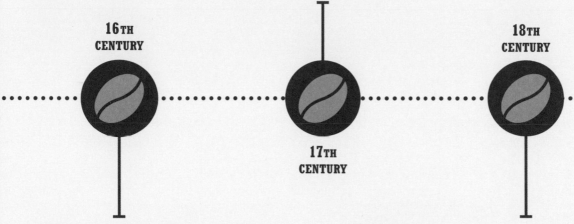

16TH CENTURY

17TH CENTURY

18TH CENTURY

- Coffee-drinking spreads throughout the Islamic world – Arabia, Egypt, Turkey and North Africa.
- Turkey opens the first coffee house outside of Arabia in 1554, called *Kiva Han,* which becomes known as the 'School of the Wise'.
- The Turks introduce coffee to Greece; the same production method is still used there to this day.

- **1714:** The Mayor of Amsterdam gives coffee as a gift to King Louis XIV of France.
- **1720:** The Portuguese take coffee to Brazil
- **1723:** A Dutch naval officer takes a seedling to the Caribbean and plants it in Martinique.
- **1750:** Rome opens its first coffee house.
- **1773:** Boston Tea Party Rebellion; coffee overtakes tea as the most popular drink in the USA.
- **1777:** Missionaries spread coffee across Central and South Americas.

COFFEE TIMELINE

A fascinating look at coffee through the ages.

- **1818:** First coffee machine – the Percolator – invented by Mr Laurnes of Paris, France.
- **1822:** First espresso machine invented by Mr Louis Bernard Rabant of France.
- Ludwig van Beethoven is said to brew his coffee with exactly 60 coffee beans.
- **1875:** The Spanish take coffee trees to Guatemala to cultivate.
- **1888:** Vincent van Gogh uses coffee motifs in his picture *Cafe Terrace at Night*.

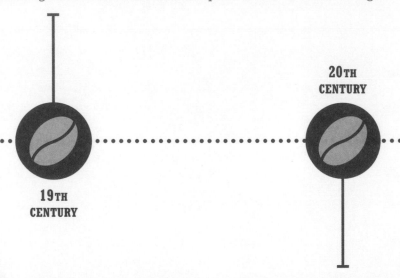

20TH CENTURY

19TH CENTURY

- **1901:** First instant coffee developed by Japanese chemist Satori Kato.
- **1903:** Decaf coffee invented by German merchant Ludwig Roselius.
- **1908:** Filter coffee created by German housewife Melita Bentz.
- **1936:** Kahlúa, the world's largest-selling coffee liqueur, is launched in Mexico.
- **1938:** Nestlé invent freeze-dried coffee in America to supply to soldiers.
- **1946:** Archilles Gaggia perfects the first espresso machine using high pressure.
- **1960:** First pump driven espresso machine produced by Faema.
- **1971:** First Starbucks opens in Seattle, Washington.
- **1982:** The Specialty Coffee Association (SCA) of America is founded.
- **1988:** The Vodka Espresso (Espresso Martini) is created by Dick Bradsell in London, England.
- **1988:** Fairtrade coffee from Mexico hits shelves in the Netherlands.

- Daily consumption of coffee worldwide reaches 1,600 million cups per day.
- 125 million people depend on coffee for their livelihood.
- One third of the tap water used for drinking in North America is used to brew daily cups of coffee.
- **2010:** Starbucks boasts revenue of $10.7 billion, making it the world's top coffee retailer.
- **2016:** As of November this year, Starbucks operates 23,768 stores globally.
- In total, approximately 150 million Americans drink 400 million cups of coffee per day (or more than 140 billion cups per year), making the United States the leading consumer of coffee in the world.

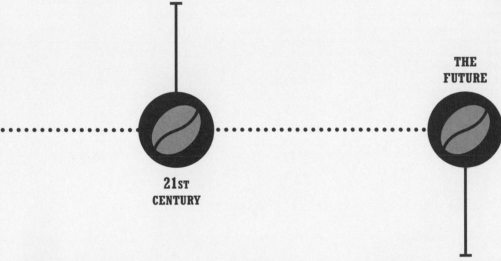

21ST CENTURY

THE FUTURE

125 million people depend on coffee for their livelihood

2.25 billion cups of coffee are drunk per day all over the world

Where does the future of coffee lie? Coffee has had an incredible journey and it's been amazing to watch its rapid progression over the past 10-plus years. The general quality and standards have sky-rocketed internationally and coffee culture his hit an all-time high. Where it will be in 10, 20, 50, 100 years we just can't tell. There are definitely concerns for coffee as a species with global warming, honey bee extinction and disease all a concern. Let's cross our fingers for coffee's survival and hope many generations get to see it thrive. I personally hope more and more people care about and appreciate coffee so that standards continue to rise, production becomes more and more sustainable and natural, and coffee farmers receive fair prices for their work – and all the while the price remains affordable for everyone to enjoy.

THE WONDERFUL WORLD OF COFFEE

Coffee is an abundantly rich and intriguing topic, brimming with stories and intrigue from historic, scientific and personal perspectives. This isn't the book to break it all down step by step – that deserves its own book, or encyclopedia even, of which there are many. This book is primarily concerned with the wealth of delicious drinks that can be made by mixing coffee with liquor.

With this in mind, before we get mixing, I'd like to give you a strong understanding of what it is that makes great coffee. This should aid you in selecting and brewing the best coffee to mix delicious drinks of a high standard. The quality of the finished cup of coffee relies hugely on the quality of the raw product and if the beans have been poorly cultivated, processed, stored or roasted, no matter how great you are on that espresso machine, you won't be able to create an immaculately complex and well-balanced cup – simply put, you can't polish a turd!

Opposite: Coffee cherries, ready to harvest. The unripened ones should ideally be left on the tree.

Above: A freshly picked harvest of coffee cherries ready to be sent for processing.

Coffee is currently classed as the world's second largest traded commodity after oil. As it is such a huge industry, it's only natural that there are different standards of coffee available, much like there are clear differences in the quality of spirits and wine to be found on the shelf in the supermarket or liquor store. In a bid to highlight the differences between bad, average, good and exceptionally good coffee, the Specialty Coffee Association of America (SCA) was formed in 1982, and it places coffee into two clear categories:

COMMODITY COFFEE The beans used to make this coffee have been produced in high volume, with little care and precision, at the lowest possible price. This type of coffee is usually produced for bigger brands and coffee chains, and will often be heavily roasted to hide imperfections, which is why you need to add a ton of sugar and milk to mask its flaws.

Then there's the type of coffee that we're interested in here to make drinks of the highest standard, which is classed as speciality coffee.

SPECIALITY COFFEE This coffee has been cultivated under strict conditions and must achieve a score of 80 points or above as stipulated by the SCA.

It is this coffee that you will find at high-quality cafes and roasteries, and it will usually be labelled with extensive details about where, when, and how the coffee was produced.

COFFEE, IN A NUTSHELL

The drink we know and love begins life on the coffee tree. Thriving in humid, tropical climates, all major producers can be found in what is classed as the coffee belt, which runs horizontally around the globe at up to 30 degrees north or south of the Equator and at altitudes between 1,000–2,000 metres above sea level.

There are many producers in each region. Here are the main ones:

LATIN AMERICA Mexico, Guatemala, El Salvador, Costa Rica, Cuba, Honduras, Nicaragua, Panama, Colombia, Brazil, Peru and Jamaica

AFRICA/ARABIA Ivory Coast, Ethiopia, Kenya, Uganda, Rwanda, Burundi, Tanzania and Yemen

ASIA PACIFIC India, Vietnam, Indonesia and Papua New Guinea

You may be surprised to know there are two specific sub-species of tree cultivated for coffee production, commonly known as Arabica and Robusta. Then there are also over 30 sub-varieties that are selected and nurtured for specific attributes desired by farmers and roasters for very different reasons – Bourbon and Typica being the two most common.

ARABICA This high-quality coffee is produced on a comparatively delicate and temperamental tree, which provides broad, complex flavour and aroma profiles.

ROBUSTA These trees are much hardier, able to withstand more varied temperatures and stronger winds, and can be grown at lower and higher altitudes. Robusta coffee also contains higher levels of caffeine and provides more crema in the finished drink, but its higher levels of bitterness and body and less complex flavours make it a lower-quality coffee than Arabica. It is generally used for instant coffee production or in cheap mass-produced blends.

The coffee bean we're familiar with is actually the seed of a fruit referred to as a cherry. The tree initially sprouts green fruit, which ripen annually and in some regions bi-annually

Right: One whole coffee cherry and one split open. Most contain two fresh seeds, known as green beans, though occasionally there might only be one.

across a range of different shades, though most varieties turn a deep burgundy at their ripest. These cherries must be picked at peak ripeness – this can be tricky for the farmers as bunches tend to develop at different times and picking under-ripe, green cherries will affect the quality of the final coffee. Once collected, farmers can select from three different processes to strip away the fruit to access the highly coveted seeds.

NATURAL/DRY PROCESS The picked fruit is spread out to dry in the sun, to release its moisture and shrivel up before being stripped dry by machines. Coffee produced this way almost always has a fuller body and deeper sweetness and is often described as "showing tropical or stewed fruits".

WASHED PROCESS This is a more modern method using machinery and water to wash away the outer layers and expose the seeds inside. Washed processed coffee generally showcases citrus fruits and has clean bright acidity with a lighter body and mouthfeel than natural processed coffee.

HONEY PROCESS A combination of the above processes, this works by stripping the skin (de-pulping) using the washed process and then leaving the beans to dry in the sun, while still coated in mucilage (flesh). In this process, the farmer has more control over the finish.

The honey process is graded in stages, from black through to red or yellow honey depending on how long the mucilage was left on after the first process and before it was stripped off. Dark honey is closer to the natural process and yellow is closer to the washed process with red sitting in the middle.

Honey-processed coffees generally have a broader flavour profile and more depth of sweetness than those produced by the other methods, which makes for a more balanced and cleaner acidity.

This may all seem fairly technical, but it is essential to know as these three processes arguably dictate more of the character that lands in your cup than the country of origin.

Most speciality coffee roasters will supply the process information on their packaged coffee.

THE ROASTERY

Once harvested, separated, dried and rested, the farmer has green beans ready to package and sell to roasters. Roasters will often have a close relationship with farmers and select the green beans on a variety of criteria suitable to the needs of their palate, brand and customers. Along with character, performance and price, many buyers will also take ethical elements into consideration.

When the green beans land in their new destination they're very bland and adding them to hot water results in a brew almost nothing like the coffee we know, so it's off to the roastery they go to be developed into the little brown nuggets of flavour we love.

While a country's sub-varieties are often classified with the same flavour profiles, they can be vastly different, so the roaster will run numerous tests and tastings to understand each batch, before roasting, blending, packaging and promoting their beans into the finished product.

One of the decisions the roaster must make is whether they are going to use the beans as single origin or as a blend.

Opposite: Green beans are loaded at source and transported to the roastery.
Above left: Coffee from different origins.
Above right: Green coffee beans going into the roaster.

SINGLE ORIGIN These beans are roasted and packaged to showcase the particular character and terroir, usually of a single farm in a single country, and will typically display complex flavours and characteristics similar to the way wines do. Speciality cafes will usually select single origin beans for their specific flavours and use a variety of gentle extraction techniques, such as cold brew (see page 40) and pour-over (see page 46).

BLENDED ORIGIN Coffees of blended origin are generally used more for commercial use and predominantly for

espresso extraction. Being a mix of different beans from different farms and countries, they tend to have big profiles that can take more heat and less precise brewing. These may also be a blend of different coffee varieties – for example a portion of Robusta may be added to lift both the caffeine and crema.

Different origins and blends exhibit completely different flavour profiles and picking the right roast can have a huge impact on the final cup, so it's worth doing your research to find the right ones that suit your requirements.

A roaster will typically do dozens of tests, roasting to different levels followed by 'cupping' (the method used for tasting a variety of coffees) to identify the best process to apply for that single origin or blend.

THE ROAST

A coffee roaster (the machine, not person) is essentially a large oven with a rotating drum, designed to heat the coffee evenly in order to draw out moisture and caramelize amino acids, fats and sugars to create the amazing flavours you'll experience in your cup.

Then there is also a person called 'a roaster' who watches over each batch to precisely control just how dark it goes, with the aim of finding the sweet spot for that particular bean. It can take as little as 10 seconds for the roast to go too far.

Roasting machines come in various styles and sizes, with the gas-heated drum style being the most popular with speciality coffee roasters. These use a fairly hands-on process and a slow approach to achieve accurate quality, whereas large commercial machines will roast hard and fast, in large volume to keep costs low.

Below left: Before fancy commercial roasters, coffee was roasted by hand. With this tricky technique, it's difficult to get accurate and consistent results.

Below right: The freshly roasted coffee is spun to stop the roasting process.

Different beans will be roasted to varying levels dependent on their style and the required flavour profile target. The freshly roasted coffee beans will then be rested to give them time to release residual carbon dioxide before being bagged to seal in the freshness.

To maximize freshness, coffee must be stored correctly. The sealed bags with one-way valves that most coffee is packaged in allows CO_2 to escape, but stops oxygen coming in which in turn prolongs its life. Once opened and exposed to oxygen, the coffee deteriorates quickly so ideally it should be used within a few days. Once open, keep it in the bag if it can be resealed; otherwise put it in an airtight jar or even use a vacuum sealer to remove the oxygen. Store it in a cool, dry, dark place (not the refrigerator).

Once the coffee has been ground, it deteriorates even more quickly so should ideally be used straight away.

Roasts fall into one of four colour categories: light, medium, medium-dark and dark. Each level will exhibit different characteristics when it reaches your cup. The lighter the roast, the more acidity increases and body decreases. The darker the roast, the more body increases, and acidity and caffeine decreases.

Above: The range of roasts from light through to dark.
Above right: From left to right, green beans, light roast, medium roast, medium-dark roast and dark roast.

LIGHT ROASTS *(Light City; Half City; Cinnamon)* Light tan in colour, these beans are best used for milder varieties of coffee and brewing. They have a very dry surface as they're not roasted long enough for the oils to be drawn through from the centre.

MEDIUM ROASTS *(City; American; Breakfast)* A milk chocolate colour, these beans have a dry surface and produce a deeper flavour. Ideal for pour-over coffee, they are often referred to as American roast because it's the roast of preference in the USA.

MEDIUM-DARK ROASTS *(Full City)* A dark chocolate colour, these beans have a light surface oil and produce a bittersweet aftertaste. Medium-dark is today's espresso roast choice for many baristas.

DARK ROASTS *(High; Continental; New Orleans; European; Espresso; Viennese; Italian; French)* These beans are intense dark chocolate with a shiny oily surface. With a longer scale, they can range from slightly dark to heavily charred. This is the traditional roast used for espresso throughout Europe.

Each sub-category will vary, so ask where a particular product lies on a roaster's scale.

SELECTING COFFEE

Bartenders rarely get the opportunity to select coffee as most venues have a pre-selected supplier. They will have to make the most of what they have or, preferably, instil a greater appreciation of coffee in order to select the highest-quality one suited to the drinks they'd like to create.

At home you have the freedom to get more creative with the coffee you want to brew.

Buying quality beans can be a bit tricky at first – it is much like stepping into a French wine cellar full of confusing labels. However it can also be great fun if you find a helpful roaster/barista to guide you.

With this help, you can pick your way through the different styles and origins to find what you like – be aware, though, that coffee is seasonal, so it will be tricky to stick to the same flavours forever. However, your palate will appreciate the opportunity to experiment.

Essentially, when selecting coffee you are looking at 7 key components:

100% ARABICA This is a must and 95+% of quality brands will only deal in 100% Arabica.

ROAST LEVEL As discussed on pages 26–27, the roast level has a huge effect on the coffee's acidity, body and complexity. You will need a roast level suited to the extraction method you are planning to use (see pages 34–49). Most brands will state the roast as espresso or filter – espresso being a darker roast to create more body; filter roast being lighter to showcase fruit, acidity and sweetness used for lighter brewing methods. You can ask the barista for more details about the depth of the roast.

COUNTRY OF ORIGIN This will give you a guide to character, but be aware that coffee can vary hugely from farm to farm within the same country.

ALTITUDE Coffee grown at a higher altitude typically produces a denser bean and has more fruit acidity and complexity, while lower elevation coffee tends to have denser body with a heavier coffee flavour.

PROCESS The processing method (Dry; Washed; Honeyed, see page 23) has a huge bearing on the outcome of the flavour and character of your coffee.

VARIETAL This will have a large bearing on the coffee's character. However, knowledge of the 30+ of these is only expected of coffee super-nerds, so find the ones you like and then use those as a guide for exploring more.

TASTING NOTES Most important of all are the tasting notes. Look for the flavours you enjoy most. Who cares if it comes from a high-elevation organic farm in Sumatra if the resulting coffee tastes like horse manure.

In the coffee notes for each recipe I have made recommendations based on my experiences, but ultimately try to familiarize yourself with the coffee available in your area and decipher its flavours and character to suit your drinks.

THE FLAVOURS OF COFFEE

Coffee tastes like coffee, right? Well, yes, but… When we delve into the depths of what makes up the flavour constituents of coffee, we open up layer upon layer of scientific intrigue. Without getting too technical, roasted coffee is full of different components – acids, sugars, fats and starches, all of which combine to create its individual character.

Extracting these components takes water, controlled temperature and, of course, time to draw out various flavours and aromas (fruity, floral, chocolate, etc) to different levels. For example, when making a French Press/cafetière coffee, a higher temperature and longer extraction time will draw out more of the bitter qualities, whereas a lower temperature and shorter extraction time will create a much easier-going, sweeter coffee.

SMELL We can break down coffee's individual flavour components much like we can with a wine or whisky. For me, however, the experience begins with the very first aromas that hit my nose, instantly sending messages to my brain along the lines of… toasted, roasted, nutty, caramel, "mmm coffee". These smells bring back memories of that invigorating lift that comes from the caffeine administered in every cup. These elements combined bring an instant smile to my face and a craving for it to hit my lips.

MOUTHFEEL When it hits my lips, it's almost a shock, because the aromas we generally associate with sweetness are now somewhat secondary to the differing sensations found through mouthfeel. With each sip you'll generally get a piquant acidity, pungent bitterness and a subtle sweetness – either dancing together in unison, or brawling in the street like drunks outside a kebab shop on a Friday night. Inhale after that first sip and you're hit with a second wave of aromas through the olfactory channel (your palate through to the inside of your nose) – perhaps apple, citrus, stone-fruit or berry notes, or floral, vegetal, herbal or smoky aromas. Essentially you are tasting every aspect of that coffee's journey from a tree top on a tropical hillside, through the hands of pickers, driers, roasters and baristas to your cup. And while each of us tastes food, drink and life in our own ways, due to our genetic make-up and past experiences, we can systematically look at and assess what we're consuming to further understand it and hopefully enjoy it even more. For some, ignorance is bliss, and that's fine too.

The wheel opposite breaks down the flavour categories to help you understand how they interact with one another. Use it to train your palate and brain to work together to identify and assess flavours. For example, if I can smell malt and nuttiness, I can assume there are caramelly, chocolatey, sugar-browning characters as these are related. Then if I sip and get a harsh, acrid mouthfeel I will get a sour acidity. Items next to each other will often (not always) be found in pairs. There can be numerous elements to each coffee, so I may get malt and nuts but also some smoke and ash leading to carbon characteristics.

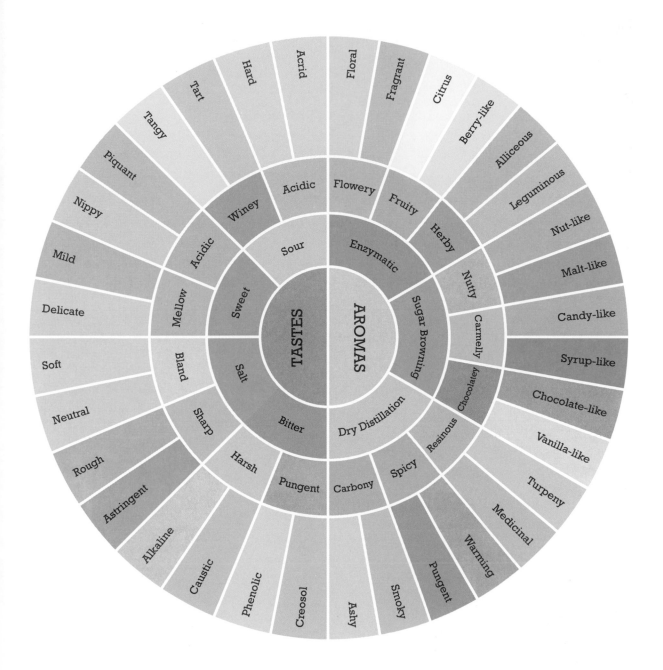

Above: This is an example of a basic flavour wheel. In 1995, the Specialty Coffee Association released a comprehensive flavour wheel, which was updated in 2016 with the World Coffee Research Center (WCR). The largest collaborative piece of research on coffee flavour has inspired a much richer vocabulary and deeper understanding of coffee flavour analysis for industry professionals. You can find the flavour wheel at https://store.sca.coffee/collections/tools/posters.

BREWING COFFEE FOR COCKTAILS

I hope from reading the previous pages you have a deeper understanding of coffee and how it is produced, and an idea of the choices on offer. The coffee you select, or are afforded to brew with, will play a hugely important role in the final result. Its origin, species, process method, roasting and freshness will ultimately dictate the quality of the drink you produce, perhaps even more so than the nuances of the brewing technique you use. Having said that, choosing the correct brewing and extracting methods and perfecting your technique will help – there's plenty of advice in the pages that follow.

Different brewing methods produce different chemical reactions within the coffee. This creates different flavour profiles, aroma, body, acidity, bitterness and depth of flavour.

There's a whole world of different options out there, besides your trusty espresso machine, to experiment with, from traditional Arabic machines to modern marvels, such as

Aeropress or the portable pocket-sized handpresso machines. I would urge you to experiment and explore different methods to find a style of coffee you can work with when designing cocktails in your bar or home.

While many of the methods can be used to create coffee for mixing cocktails, there are two main extraction methods I recommend.

ESPRESSO is the go-to option in bars. It gives you delicious, robust coffee that can be used in countless recipes and a fast brew time when compared with many other methods (however, it does have its drawbacks too). Nespresso or similar pod coffee-makers also fall under this heading. Although not as versatile, they have a number of other advantages such as their compact size, speed and

Left: Brewing fresh espresso.

consistency. See pages 36–39 for how to achieve good results with your espresso machine.

COLD BREW Espresso is and has been for a long time now by far and away the most popular method of extraction used for coffee cocktails. However, slowly but surely bartenders and home brewers everywhere are and will be making the leap from espresso to immersion cold brew over the coming years. ICB is the future of coffee cocktails in bars!

By using the immersion cold brew method (see pages 40–43), you can easily create large, consistent batches of well-balanced coffee with a long shelf life that can be served in an instant. These are all characteristics that make it hugely appealing for bar use. I can't recommend its usage enough.

Above: Whatever method or machine you use to brew your coffee, a systematic, clean, consistent approach will reap the best results.

Tips and techniques
Here are my tips for achieving good results, but remember practice makes perfect and in time you will improve your results and learn from your mistakes:

• Measure and weigh the quantities of both water and coffee accurately.
• Check that temperatures are within the recommended ranges.
• Sterilize tools and equipment.
• Take notes. This way you can use a process of elimination to progress with the best results, rather than going around in circles.

Watch and learn
Don't be afraid to grab a seat at the counter of your favourite cafe, order a brew, watch, ask and learn first hand from a pro. Professional baristas are usually proud coffee geeks, who love their craft and generally won't hesitate to share with those who ask. Just make sure you pick a quiet time of their day and leave a generous tip.

Finally, remember if you treat your coffee with love, it'll love you back and you'll reap the rewards.

EXTRACTION

There are dozens of extraction methods to choose from when brewing your coffee. From cold drip or Chemex, to Moka pot or syphon. When combined with different beans, roasts and ratios, there are infinite possibilities. In speciality coffee cafes, the barista will be considering all of these elements with every serve; at home, however, these elements all rely on you.

To get the best results you will need to use a methodical process of measurement and experimentation, making small adjustments as you go, towards creating that perfect, consistent coffee you love to drink.

In the following pages I offer a few key tips for brewing, using the four main extraction methods used throughout this book: espresso, cold brew, French press and pour-over, and

Below left: Roasted coffee beans heading into the burr grinder.
Below right: Freshly ground coffee on its way to the espresso machine.

there's also a section on pod coffee for the Nespresso users. I have purposefully left out a number of other methods such as Aeropress and Moka as I don't find them to be particularly efficient for coffee cocktails.

GRINDING How the coffee has been ground is essential to the extraction process, but is often overlooked. Different methods of brewing have different contact requirements with the ground coffee and each results in different flavours but not always in a good way. For example, with espresso the water meets the ground coffee for a mere 15–30 seconds, meaning the grinds need to be fine

in order for the water to penetrate and draw out the flavour, aroma and texture quickly. This is also helped by the pressure at which the water is pumped through the machine, which creates the lovely smooth crema we expect and love with espresso. If your grind is too coarse, it won't extract enough from the coffee (under-extraction) and if too fine it will over-extract the body and flavour components. So grinding must be accurate for all different methods to achieve the best results with the beans you have.

To grind accurately, you will need a conical burr grinder (see page 14), as they are the most precise and consistent. These range from big commercial machines to compact home versions that can be found at any electrical appliance store. Stay away from spinning blade grinders, which are highly inaccurate and inefficient.

Ideally, grind the coffee only as needed, as it will rapidly deteriorate through oxidation once ground. Store coffee in a cool dark place, in an airtight container, for no more than a few days. Do not refrigerate it.

It takes a little experimentation to get to grips with finding the best grind settings for different brewing methods, so I recommend you take notes so that you can keep track of results and eliminate repeat mistakes.

Below: From fine to coarse, it's important to use the correct type of ground coffee for the extraction method you are using. Not pictured here is 'Extra Fine', which is used for Turkish-style extraction.

FINE	**MEDIUM-FINE**	**MEDIUM**	**COARSE**	**WHOLE BEANS**
Espresso	Aeropress	Chemex	Siphon	
	Moka	Pour-over	Cold brew	
			French Press	

ESPRESSO EXTRACTION

Espresso machines were created in Italy in the late 1940s to serve quality coffee to order for guests who were on the fly. It soon took off and became the number one method for coffee lovers worldwide. Today it is the most popular style of coffee used for cocktails and the espresso machine has become an essential addition to most bars – and for good reason. Nothing perks up a good night out like a double espresso, let alone an Espresso Martini, or a host of other invigorating, caffeine-laced drinks that can be made using Italy's finest export.

There are pros and cons to serving espresso coffees in bars. The pros include the delicious, deep, pungent, complex and concentrated coffee you can achieve, the speed of producing it compared to other methods, the familiarity for both staff and guests and, of course, that rich crema.

The cons, however, are the bulky size of the machine that takes up precious space in the bar, the often-temperamental results, the speed in comparison to pouring something from a bottle and the laborious clean-up at the end of each night. The biggest downfalls, however, tend to be the quality of the coffee and lack of staff training.

QUALITY OF COFFEE No matter how well you maintain your machine and perform your extraction, you can only affect the original coffee so much and in the end its flaws will show through if it is poor quality.

TRAINING A lack of quality training can cause huge inconsistencies between staff members and often poor results. I cannot urge bar management enough when it comes to training and testing staff extensively to ensure they are creating quality coffee on a consistent level. Instil in them a passion to deliver coffee of the highest standard at all times!

Left and opposite: There's something pretty special about that magical moment when good-quality coffee drips from the espresso machine into your cup. The colours, aromas, textures and temperatures are spellbinding.

Tips and techniques

Assuming you already have an espresso machine, grinder, tamp tool, etc, and know how to use them, here are a few tips and techniques to help you get the best possible results from your machine.

• Don't overload the grinder's hopper with more beans than you will use in one day.

• Grind the coffee as you need it, not before.

• After removing the portafilter, flush water through the group head for 2–3 seconds to rinse out any unwanted residue left over from previous extractions.

• Empty the portafilter and wipe it to remove any residual coffee.

• Ideally, weigh the coffee to obtain a precise quantity and give you consistency. If this isn't possible, fill the portafilter basket and scrape the coffee to ensure it is evenly flush.

• If the coffee is sitting unevenly you can tap it with your hand to shuffle it over, but do not tap it with the tamping tool.

• Place the portafilter on the bench and press it evenly with the tamp. It is important not to press it to one side.

• Press the tamp down snugly, lightly twisting it left and right to polish the pressed coffee.

• Use your hand to wipe away any excess grinds from the edge to ensure they don't fall inside the basket.

• Once you add the portafilter into the machine, you need to run the extraction straight away as leaving it will start to cook the grinds prematurely.

• Watch the extraction. This is the moment of truth! Too fast will mean under-extracted coffee, too slow means burnt, bitter, over-extracted coffee. You need to get the flow rate just right (see previous page).

Below: Carefully tamping the coffee creates a great espresso.

Below: An example of a bad tamp!

Above: The milk is heated and aerated.

Above: Pouring a perfect Flat White.

• The grind size and tamp pressure will affect this process the most, so you will need to adjust these to get the results best suited to your machine.

• Extract for between 20–30 seconds. If you watch the extraction you will see the colour start to lighten and the flow change. This signifies the extraction is complete.

• Examine the extracted crema. Ideally, you want nice, even colouring without dark or light patches.

• When it comes to steaming and pouring milk for coffee, it is somewhat of a delicate art form. Achieving good texture requires precise placement and control of the steam wand into the jug to create a flowing whirlpool followed by a process called stretching the milk to fill it with micro bubbles while it is heated.

• Be gentle and smooth and don't over-stimulate it.

• The correct temperature can be achieved by touching the base of the jug to judge the heat, which comes from experience.

• It is better to under-heat rather than over-heat, as once the milk is scorched the flavour changes to the detriment of your coffee.

• Finally, keep your machine and tools clean and tidy at all times. Backwash it with both water and espresso shampoo regularly. Remember, if you look after your machine, it'll look after you!

COLD BREW EXTRACTION

I'm a firm believer (preacher) in the benefits of cold brew coffee for making cocktails in both bars and at home, and slowly but surely others are catching on to the quality and convenience of this method.

In the cold brew technique, time rather than heat is used to extract the flavours and aromas from the coffee and this makes for a hugely different, yet equally delicious result. With more sweetness and less acidity and bitterness, cold brew is very moreish and versatile, allowing it to be served in an infinite number of ways.

There are a number of different methods for cold brew extraction, all of which are best suited to single origin Arabica (see page 22) and require a coarsely ground coffee (see page 35) similar to that used for French press/cafetière coffee, if not even coarser. The ratio of coffee to water you use is a matter of personal preference. I tend to extract at a concentrated level and add water to soften it, as needed.

COLD DRIP COFFEE

Water is slowly dripped through the coffee grinds into a chamber below, picking up the coffee's character along the way. You'll require a fairly high-tech and delicate piece of kit called a cold drip tower (see right).

Room temperature or iced water is placed in the top chamber above a middle compartment containing ground coffee. The top chamber has a flow regulator, which is

adjusted to allow water to slowly drip over the coffee, which then drains through a filter into an empty vessel at the bottom. A coarse grind similar to that used for immersion cold brew or French press /cafetière is recommended. Ratio-wise it's up to you, dependent on how

Right: A cold drip tower. Water is slowly gravity-fed through the coffee to produce cold drip coffee.

strong you want your coffee – 1:10 is great for a ready-to-drink brew, but I tend to do a 1:7 concentrate to use for cocktails.

The length of time needed for a full process is dependent on the volume of water your dripper holds and how fast you set the valve. I tend to do 2 litres/66 oz water, 280 g/10 oz coffee with a drip rate set to 1 drip per 1.5 seconds (40 per minute). This delivers a complex but strong concentrate that you can dilute down further if you want to soften it.

The second method, and my personal favourite for home and bar use, is the immersion method.

THE IMMERSION METHOD

This basically translates to "slow infusion batching". To perform this method, simply add a large quantity of coarsely ground coffee into a large container of water and leave it to slowly absorb its character. Once the desired result is reached, strain/filter it to separate the water from the coffee granules.

The grind size and coffee to water ratios are very important here and so is the overall immersion time. Different filters will also give you different results that require slight adjustments. I use the formulas given right and overleaf as a base and then adjust them to suit different roasts of different origins.

Overall I've found that using this method at these ratios creates the perfect strength coffee for mixing cocktails where in the past I would have simply used espresso. Once

you've experimented to achieve the results you want, you'll be a pro in no time at all.

TODDY SYSTEM For this method the top hopper is loaded with coarsely ground coffee and cold water to a 1:5 ratio (250 g/9 oz coffee x 1,250 g/43 oz mineral water). Depending on the roast I tend to leave it for 16–18 hours. The plastic hopper comes with a built-in but removable filter, so when it's ready, simply remove the bung in the bottom with it sitting over the glass base and allow the coffee to drain. This takes about 10–15 minutes and yields around 1 litre/33 oz of concentrated cold brew. I've found this to be the easiest and most consistent method.

Right: The Toddy Immersion System. Coffee and water are infused in the plastic hopper. When ready, the bung is removed and the cold brew dribbles through the filter into the glass jug below.

Above: Using The Toddy System, the coffee has just been added to the water and is slowly infusing.

FRENCH PRESS FILTER The French Press/cafetière method is great for home brewing smaller batches when you don't have fancy filters available. The stainless steel filter is also a little more open than the others, changing the ratio to around 1:6 (166 g/6 oz coffee x 1 litre/33 oz water). Allow it to sit for 16 hours, then press down the plunger and pour out the filtered cold brew. This filter will leave you with an oilier and grittier coffee, so don't be surprised by the cloudiness.

All of these methods will give you strong concentrated coffee. I find 30 ml/1 oz at these strengths matches up well to 30 ml/1 oz of espresso, yet has less acidity and bitterness, helping create super-smooth drinks. You can also easily compensate for the different balance in cocktails by using other ingredients such as bitters.

STORAGE

Bottle your cold brew and store it in the refrigerator – it should have a shelf-life of up to two weeks, making it absolutely perfect for both bar and home use. It's lovely served over ice, or with chilled water added to lengthen it out to a longer drink, and also works well with different types of milk – from cow's milk to coconut milk. And if you want a hot coffee on the go, simply add boiling water to a shot of cold brew and you're away laughing.

ROAST

Typically, when making cold brew to drink on its own I use a light/medium filter coffee roast to bring out more fruit flavours and less acid. However, for cocktail use I've found darker espresso roasts tend to work better as they deliver the body and acidity we are accustomed to when using espresso.

PAPER AND SUPERBAG FILTERS For this method, add both the coarsely ground coffee and cold water to a large jar at a 1:5 ratio (250 g/9 oz coffee to 1,250 ml/43 oz mineral water). Depending on the roast, I tend to leave it for 18–20 hours as the fine paper filter tends to strip out more flavour than the Toddy system and the extra time will help compensate for that. Make sure you rinse the filter thoroughly with water first to remove paper fibres and also open up the pores a little. The superbag is a little less extracting, so 17–19 hours should be fine.

These methods are also a lot slower to drain than the Toddy filter, so set it aside and give it time to drain completely without forcing it. They also yield around 1 litre/33 oz of concentrated cold brew.

Top left: Superbag filter step 1
Top right: Superbag filter step 2
Bottom left: Coarsely ground coffee
Bottom right: French Press/cafetière filter method

FRENCH PRESS EXTRACTION

The trusty old coffee plunger, also known as the French Press or cafetière, has been a staple for brewing coffee at home for many generations, as well as being a quick and easy way to produce coffee for a group of friends in less than 10 minutes with little fuss. However it's often made poorly by throwing ingredients together without care. You need to be accurate with measures, timing and temperatures to get the best flavours out of your coffee. Here are my instructions for a 2-cup brew...

For 2 servings

32 g/1⅛ oz coarse ground coffee

100 g/3½ oz room-temperature mineral water

400 g/14 oz boiled water (plus 200 g/7 oz for preheating)

Once the kettle has boiled, pour approximately 200 g/7 oz of water into your French Press/cafetière to preheat it. Swirl and discard. You can also preheat your cups now.

Add the coffee and saturate it with the mineral water, then allow it to settle for 30 seconds. This will 'bloom' the coffee allowing CO_2 to evaporate and also stop the coffee being scorched when you add your hot water.

Give it a quick stir and then add 400g/14 oz of hot water from the kettle (picture opposite, top right). Put the lid on. Leave to brew for 4 minutes.

Depress the plunger slowly and steadily (picture opposite, bottom left).

Pour and enjoy.

Barista tips

• Pour all the coffee off immediately to prevent over-extraction that can cause bitterness.

• Select a quality single-origin coffee with characteristics you enjoy. Different styles of coffee will affect your ratios so use trial and error to find best results.

• The ideal water temperature to use is 96°C/204°F.

POUR-OVER EXTRACTION

Pour-over filter brewed coffee such as V60 (pictured) and Chemex have absolutely boomed in popularity over the past few years. Coffee geeks and baristas have taken a huge shine to these styles for a number of reasons – the main one being that they're a much gentler extraction method than espresso or stovetop, so are great for showcasing the more delicate and subtle character of 100% Arabica Single Origin coffees. The ratios, water temperature and coffee contact can all be manipulated, which allows the barista to deliver coffee that is light, clean and easy-going. It's a very methodical process and essential to get your weight ratios correct.

16 g/½ oz medium/coarse ground coffee

250 g/9 oz boiled water (ideal temperature is 96°C/205°F) plus 100–200 g/3½–7oz for preheating

Once the kettle has boiled, pour approximately 100–200 g/3½–7oz of water through the filter and into your coffee mug or serving jug, swirl and discard. This will rinse the filter and preheat your vessel.

Add the coffee to the filter and saturate it with 50g/1¾ oz of water, then wait 20 seconds. This is called blooming as it allows trapped CO_2 to escape the coffee, which creates bitter carbonic acid (picture opposite, top right).

Pour in the remaining 200 g/7 oz of water in a slow circular motion to ensure an even extraction (pictures opposite, bottom left and right). Wait for it to drain through.

Serve and enjoy!

Barista tip This is a great method to make a brew to share with friends. I personally don't tend to use it too often for cocktails as it's a little slow and laborious.

POD COFFEE EXTRACTION

While it's not the only single-serve pod coffee available on the market, Nespresso seemingly exploded out of nowhere and has revolutionized home and office brewing, becoming the market leader by far. In recent years, pod coffee has really boomed internationally.

Many people swear by it, others deplore it. Personally I sit on the fence; it has its pros and cons. It's a great option for small spaces, including bars, making it possible to produce coffee with minimum fuss and mess and its extraction quality far outweighs any instant coffee and actually blows away many commercial coffee shops too. While the flavour profile pales in comparison to high-quality, speciality coffee made by an experienced barista, it more than makes up for it with both consistency and convenience. This makes it ideal for using to mix cocktails and mocktails, so I think we'll see people getting a lot more creative with it in coming years both at home and in bars.

The negative side is of course the excessive pollution pod coffees create. Unable to be recycled at a typical plant, they need to be sent directly back to the producer, which is counterintuitive to the convenience they provide in the first place. This proves to be a deal-buster for many in this day and age of consumer consciousness in regards to environmental issues.

Single-serve pod coffee is slowly becoming the instant coffee of our age. And if it gets you into coffee and ensures I get a decent cup when visiting, then sure, go for it... and it will likely lead you on the path to better coffee in the long run.

I have three tips to offer pod coffee users:

• Keep your water tank low so you're always using fresh quality water.

• Keep your machine clean. Run a little water through it before each extraction to clear any old residue.

• If you like the convenience of pod coffee, consider switching to cold brew (see page 40). You can mix a 2-litre/66 oz batch that will see you through 1–2 weeks, providing great flavour, consistency and minimal fuss with each serve!

Below and opposite: A coffee pod machine and pods.

COCKTAIL FUNDAMENTALS

What are cocktails? Yes, they are mixed alcoholic beverages using any number of different ingredients, but they can be so much more than that! Creating a good cocktail is a special moment, allowing bartenders to showcase their skill and the personality of both themselves and their venue to their guests.

A PERFECT G&T

Take a simple Gin & Tonic. While a guest may be able to purchase one at any bar, anywhere in the world, there can be a huge difference from one to the next, even when using essentially the same four ingredients – gin, tonic, garnish and ice.

The glassware can make a huge difference to the look and feel, not to mention the expression of aroma. The shape, quality and volume of ice will affect the aesthetic, temperature and flavour from start to finish. That seemingly insignificant piece of citrus, sadly dropped on the top at the end, could and should be squeezed to release its juices and essential oils into the drink, enhancing both flavour and aroma, particularly if it appropriately matches the characteristics of the chosen gin.

In fact, is citrus even a correct match to the gin you're pouring, or is there something else better suited like cucumber or fresh basil?

And, finally, the different types and ratio of both the gin and tonic will affect the experience hugely. Too much gin can be uncomfortably strong; too much tonic and the gin is lost. Do their flavours match up well and are they suited to the guest's palate?

MADE TO ORDER

Every cocktail should be served to suit that particular guest at that particular moment in time, with the aim of giving them that special "wow" feeling that puts a smile on their face and a spring in their step. "Cocktails are liquid happiness!"

THE RIGHT BALANCE

The structure of a great cocktail relies on a balance of contrasts – strong versus weak, sweet versus sour and/or bitter and sometimes salty or savoury. When perfectly aligned, all of these contrasts work together in a beautiful balancing act to create the drinks we know and love.

Classic cocktails tend to fit within specific formulas using the above elements, and the great thing about these formulas is that the ingredients within are all very interchangeable, giving us almost endless possibilities for variations. So depending on the flavours of your drink, you can swap ingredients out for other like-minded ones – for example, regular white sugar syrup can be swapped for brown sugar, maple, honey, agave or other flavoured syrups, for example.

You can't always swap out quantities equally due to the different sugar and flavour levels each ingredient has, but the measurements will be close and you'll be able to taste and adjust very easily. And you will need to, as my coffee will be different to yours, as will your ice, and often various other elements.

Many cocktail recipes are reconfigurations of each other's formulas, so once you understand the structures applied you'll be able to do your own twists and tweaks to the drinks in this book, along with other favourites, just like a pro.

INGREDIENTS

Choose quality over quantity. Your drink is only as good as its weakest ingredient, so do your best to use the best products possible within your budget. I recommend using fresh natural ingredients rather than cheap, mass-produced items. For example, fresh raspberries or a natural raspberry purée will always taste better than any syrup made with 5% raspberry, corn syrup, E512 and a ton of sugar. The same goes for espresso – a shot precisely extracted using good-quality roasted beans from a reliable source will be infinitely better than your typical corporate chain coffee shot.

Taste and adjust as you go to find balance. This can be done by simply stirring the ingredients and then dropping a single drop from the spoon on to the back of your hand and tasting it to check its balance.

Lastly, and most importantly of all, have fun! Cocktails are all about enjoyment for everyone involved, including the bartender. If you're not having fun, you're doing something wrong.

Good luck!

1 SHAKEN

Shaken cocktails made with coffee create that lovely, fluffy, aerated crema most famously associated with the Espresso Martini. With the recent boom in coffee culture internationally, bars have finally been encouraged to have well-equipped coffee machines at hand, along with the skills needed to use them. This has led to a huge rise in the popularity of coffee cocktails over the past few years and, in particular, for the infamous Espresso Martini.

Bartender's tips

• For any shaken cocktail, always chill the glass you plan to serve it in. To do this, simply add cubed or crushed ice to it and set it to one side while you mix the cocktail.

• Pour the ingredients into the small part of the shaker, then fill it to the top with ice. Do not add the ice before the ingredients.

• Always shake with cubed ice. Shake hard for approximately 10 seconds until you get a frost forming on the outside of the shaker.

• Open your shaker and then either remove and refresh the ice (if required) or drain off the water in the glass before straining in the cocktail.

• Most iced cocktails require straining over fresh ice, rather than using the ice from the shaker.

• Cocktails "served up" (ie. with no ice) require double straining. Use a hawthorne strainer, but use a mesh basket to remove ice shards and other ingredient pulp.

ESPRESSO MARTINI

Originally called The Pharmaceutical Stimulant and the Vodka Espresso, the infamous Espresso Martini was created at Fred's Club, London, in the late 1980s by Dick Bradsell, considered to be one of the most influential bartenders of the modern era. When a model approached him and asked for "something to wake me up, and f*** me up," Dick's response was to combine vodka, fresh espresso, coffee liqueur and sugar, and shake it into a frothy mix of bittersweet invigoration, strained into an elegant glass. When shaken, the natural oils create that beautiful, frothy crema on top and leave a velvety smooth elegance below. As with any cocktail, quality ingredients make for a better drink. Always draw the fresh espresso first so that it has time to cool and add the other ingredients before the ice hits the shaker. This is an easy drink to twist into something unique by substituting the vodka, sugar, liqueur or glass for other similar products. Just ensure you get that bitter-sweet-strong balance spot on. Dick Bradsell sadly passed away in 2016. A quiet, heads-down, tail-up character, Dick tended to let his drinks do the talking. His best drinks have a simplicity that clicks and makes bartenders ponder, "Why didn't I think of that?" Cheers to Dick Bradsell and the Espresso Martini!

40 ml/1⅓ oz vodka
30 ml/1 oz fresh espresso
20 ml/⅔ oz coffee liqueur
10 ml/⅓ oz sugar syrup

To garnish
3 coffee beans

Add the ingredients to a cocktail shaker, shake with cubed ice and double strain into a chilled Martini or coupette glass. Garnish with coffee beans.

For the sugar syrup: add 500 ml/17 oz of boiling water to 1 kg/5 cups soft brown sugar, stir and allow to dissolve. Leave to cool. Add to a sterilized bottle and refrigerate for up to 4 months.

COFFEE Use house espresso, naturally, but experimenting with cold brew brings great results too.

LIQUOR Vodka-wise, take your pick from the many quality brands on the market. Personally, I'm a big fan of Ketel One – it's very smooth, but has a full-grain character that stands up well to the other ingredients and pairs really well with espresso.

MILK & COOKIES

The classic combination of milk and cookies is a fond childhood memory for me. I've put an adult spin on it with the addition of coffee and liquor. Ideally, shake it in the bottle you plan to serve it in or, alternatively, in a cocktail shaker with no ice works well too.

45 ml/1½ oz whisky/whiskey
30 ml/1 oz cold brew coffee
15 ml/½ oz golden syrup
90 ml/3 oz milk (dairy or nut milks can all work well)

To serve
Cookies (optional)

Add the ingredients to a chilled 300 ml/10 oz bottle and shake. Serve with a couple of cookies on the side, if you like.

COFFEE A double shot of house espresso or cold brew works fine. I like to add it after shaking the other ingredients to watch it cascade through the milk. To get even more foam, shake it a second time.

LIQUOR I've left this super-simple recipe open-ended so you can add whichever whisky or whiskey you prefer, be that a blended Scotch, Single Malt, Blended Malt, Irish, Canadian or American. It's a versatile drink open to interpretation. Hell, vodka, rum, tequila, or brandy can all potentially work well in this drink!

BIG BREW

This is designed for ease, when you need to make multiple Espresso Martini-style drinks and are far too busy socializing to be trapped in the kitchen mixing cocktails. You simply prepare a bottle in advance that gives you 10 servings, then refrigerate it. When your guests arrive, take it out, shake and serve.

For 10 servings
450 ml/15 oz vodka
300 ml/10 oz fresh cold brew coffee
150 ml/5 oz coffee liqueur
85 ml/2¾ oz sugar syrup
  (see page 55)
10 dashes Angostura Bitters
  (optional)

To garnish
Coffee beans
A sprinkle of nutmeg powder
  per serve (optional)

Add the ingredients to a 1 litre/33 oz bottle for 10 servings. When ready to serve, shake individual 100 ml/3¼ oz measures with cubed ice in a cocktail shaker or, alternatively, give the bottle a good shake, then pour over ice straight into the glasses. Garnish with coffee beans and nutmeg, if using.

COFFEE My preference is for a rich cold brew, such as a Guatemalan or Colombian medium roast.

LIQUOR Vodka-wise, go with your favourite brand. The optional bitters adds a touch of complexity and helps balance the sweetness, but isn't essential.

COFFEE & A CUBAN

If you like coffee, rum, cigars and chocolate half as much as I do, then this one is for you. It's such a simple recipe, yet it works so well and just makes sense. On a visit to Cuba, I lost count of how many times I indulged in espresso and rum alongside a fine Cuban cigar. It eventually inspired me to bring the three even closer together, with a touch of sugar to round out the mouthfeel and a little salted dark chocolate served on the side. This one should be on every dad's Father's Day list.

45 ml/1½ oz aged Cuban rum
30 ml/1 oz espresso
7.5 ml/¼ oz brown sugar syrup
  (see page 55)

To garnish
Grated nutmeg

To serve
Dark chocolate (70 per cent
  cocoa solids)
Sea salt
Cigar (optional)

Add the ingredients to a cocktail shaker, shake with cubed ice and double strain into a chilled rocks glass with no ice. Garnish, and serve with dark chocolate sprinkled with sea salt and your cigar of choice, if desired.

COFFEE A good-quality espresso works well, but you can also use a full-flavoured cold brew such as a Guatemalan, Colombian or Cuban.

LIQUOR Choose a nice, moderately aged Cuban-style rum. I've used Matusalem Reserve and Solera 15, but Bacardi 8 and Havana 7 also work well.

SUPER STOUT

You'd be forgiven for thinking this is a half pint of Ireland's finest! It's actually the result of my warped mind re-imagining an Irish coffee. I'm a huge fan of an ice-cold Guinness, and in this killer recipe I've combined it with coffee and whiskey to transform it into a Super Stout. It's bound to rub many a Guinness purist up the wrong way, but it's worth it for the delicious result. The Guinness replaces the use of cream to retain a velvety texture.

35 ml/1¼ oz Irish whiskey

90 ml/3 oz Fig & Hazelnut cold brew coffee (see page 191), diluted to half strength

15 ml/½ oz sugar syrup (see page 55)

90 ml/3 oz Guinness Irish stout

To garnish
Light sprinkle of grated nutmeg

Add the whiskey, coffee and sugar syrup into a cocktail shaker, shake with cubed ice and strain into a chilled Guinness half pint glass. Top with Guinness poured from a height to invigorate the crema and create a foamy texture. Garnish with a sprinkling of grated nutmeg.

COFFEE A chocolatey medium dark roasted Colombian, Guatemalan or Brazilian works well with both the whiskey and stout. It needs diluting to half-strength to deliver the volume but not the power of full-strength cold brew. Regular cold brew works fine here, but using the Fig & Hazelnut recipe from page 191 takes it to a whole new level.

LIQUOR Choose a full-bodied Irish whiskey such as Tullamore Dew, Roe & Co, Jameson Black Barrel or Jameson Bold, which will all stand up to both the coffee and the stout.

FRENCH PRESS MARTINI

A super-simple twist on the Espresso Martini, I first created this cocktail at a house party in Queenstown, New Zealand, back in 2008, in the lead up to a concert. With a room full of thirsty friends, I decided to whip up a round of coffee cocktails to energize everyone for the evening ahead. With no espresso machine or coffee liqueur at hand, I improvised by making a batch of spiced, French Press/cafetière coffee. I simply stirred cocoa powder, Chinese five spice powder and caster/superfine sugar into a standard coffee and water mix. By combining 60 ml/2 oz of this mixture with 45 ml/1½ of vodka (x 6) in a large (sterilized) pickling jar, I was able to quickly knock out enough drinks to get everybody on form ready for a big night ahead.

For 20 servings
64 g/2⅓ oz coarsely ground coffee
150 g/¾ cup caster/superfine
  sugar
½ tsp cocoa powder
¼ tsp Chinese 5 spice powder
  or cinnamon
900 ml/30 oz boiling water
1 litre/33 oz vodka

To garnish
Chinese 5 spice powder

Combine all the ingredients, except the vodka and Chinese 5 spice, in a large French press/cafetière and leave it to stand for 4 minutes. Stir, then plunge and pour into a new jug or bottle to stop the infusion.

Add 60 ml/2 oz of the mixture and 45 ml/1½ oz vodka to a cocktail shaker, fill with cubed ice and shake hard. Strain into chilled Champagne flutes, Martini glasses or similar. Garnish with a dash of Chinese 5 spice powder.

COFFEE This recipe simply calls for whatever ground coffee you have in the cupboard at home.

LIQUOR Vodka-wise, go with your favourite brand. Vanilla vodka and gold or spiced rum also work really well in this recipe.

THE ITALIAN SECRET

This cocktail is inspired by the Southern Italian tradition of adding a lemon slice to strong Italian roast coffee to lighten it up and complement its bitter notes – something few people outside Italy have caught on to. Here, I've added another secret ingredient – a little liquor – and no one will be the wiser while you sip it discreetly from a coffee glass.

15 ml/½ oz grappa
15 ml/½ oz hazelnut liqueur
15 ml/½ oz Averna Digestivo
60 ml/2 oz mocha pot coffee

To garnish
Lemon twist

Add the ingredients to a cocktail shaker, shake hard with cubed ice and double strain into a small coffee glass. Garnish with a lemon twist, and serve with biscotti and toasted hazelnuts, if you like.

COFFEE The classic stove-top moka pot is ideal for this drink, but strong espresso can work well also.

LIQUOR Grappa-wise I like something aged and nutty, like Cocchi Grappa Dorée. For the hazelnut liqueur, Frangelico works well but my favourite is Nocello, which hails from the north-east of Italy.

UN-FIG-EDIBLE

Enjoy a coming together of coffee, Spanish brandy and some exquisite Pedro Ximénez vermouth from Jerez, Spain. This is enhanced with the richness of fig jam and complemented with Aphrodite Bitters, which deliver coffee, cacao, ginger, chilli/chili, allspice and more, making for a highly complex cold brew Martini you won't ever fig-et.

40 ml/1⅓ oz Spanish brandy
20 ml/⅔ oz Lustau Pedro Ximénez sherry sweet vermouth
40 ml/1⅓ oz cold brew coffee
1 tsp fig jam
3 dashes Dr. Adam Elmegirab's Aphrodite Bitters

To garnish
½ fresh winter fig

Add the ingredients to a cocktail shaker and shake with cubed ice, then double strain into a chilled Martini glass. Garnish with half a fresh winter fig.

COFFEE I use a lighter roast Ethiopian origin Arabica for this drink, brewed at a 6:1 ratio (see pages 40–43), showcasing bright acidity and dried stone fruit character.

LIQUOR The fruitiness and nuttiness of Torres 10-year Spanish brandy pairs exceptionally well with the sherry vermouth and it is enhanced with the bitters' poignant balance of spices.

BEETS BY J

Somewhat surprisingly, beetroot tends to work really well with coffee – in fact, beetroot lattes can occasionally be spotted on the menus of creative cafes. This twist on a sour recipe is whisky forward, with the coffee just sliding sneakily in at the side.

45 ml/1½ oz blended Scotch whisky
15 ml/½ oz Drambuie
15 ml/½ oz cold brew coffee
30 ml/1 oz beetroot juice
15 ml/½ oz lemon juice
15 ml/½ oz egg white
7.5 ml/¼ oz hibiscus syrup
Dash of The Bitter Truth Creole Bitters

To garnish
A raspberry
Dehydrated raspberry powder

Add the ingredients to a cocktail shaker, shake with cubed ice and double strain into a chilled fluted glass. Garnish with a raspberry and raspberry powder.

COFFEE The coffee plays a supporting role to the other robust flavours in this drink. I chose a lighter roast with a bright acidity and dried stone fruit character.

LIQUOR A quality medium-bodied blended Scotch whisky, such as Johnnie Walker Gold Label, Chivas 12 or Dewar's 8, is best suited to this cocktail.

GOLDEN VELVET

Like liquid gold literally dancing on your tongue, this luxurious after-dinner extravagance is a great one to pull out to impress friends. The coffee element is quite light, so it's a good late-night option that won't keep you awake.

37.5 ml/1¼ oz salted caramel vodka

15 ml/½ oz Licor 43

7.5 ml/¼ oz banana liqueur

30 ml/1 oz half & half (see page 204)

15 ml/½ oz cold brew coffee

Dash coffee bitters (see page 192)

Pinch gold dust

To garnish

Spray the glass with Licor 43, then coat in a mixture of gold dust, gold flake and popping candy

To prepare the glass: chill a flute glass and coat with gold dust (see left).

To make the cocktail: add the ingredients to a cocktail shaker, shake hard with cubed ice and double strain into the glass. Garnish with more gold flakes.

COFFEE To match the velvety smooth texture of this drink, you need a light coffee with low bitterness. I use a nutty Indonesian single origin cold brew.

LIQUOR I used Stolichnaya Salted Caramel vodka. If it's not available, then any vanilla vodka works well as a substitute. Licor 43 is a delicious spiced vanilla and orange liqueur from Spain.

COFFEE CHERRY

This drink was inspired by the scarlet red-ripened coffee cherries that contain hidden coffee seeds. The raw crispness of Cachaça is paired with raspberry and lemon, and the coffee is administered by adding coffee ice, which slowly melts into the drink to impart its flavour in a ripple effect. Cascara is the dried-up skin of the coffee cherry, which normally goes to waste. Paired with bee pollen in a syrup, it delivers a warm, honeyed tamarind complexity.

Large coffee ice sphere
(see page 188)
45 ml/1½ oz Cachaça
10 ml/⅓ oz Cherry Heering liqueur
30 ml/1 oz lemon juice
30 ml/1 oz raspberry purée
15 ml/½ oz cascara and bee pollen
syrup (see below)
15 ml/½ oz egg white (optional)
Dash of Peychaud's Bitters

To garnish
Gold flakes
Bee pollen

Cascara and bee pollen syrup
20 g/¾ oz bee pollen
500 ml/17 oz mineral water
500 g/2½ cups white sugar
50 g/1¾ oz cascara/dried coffee
cherries
0.5 g citric acid

For the cascara and bee pollen syrup: in a large saucepan, toast the bee pollen, add the rest of the ingredients and bring to the boil. Stir until the sugar and bee pollen dissolve. Remove from heat and allow to cool, then filter through a mesh strainer. Bottle and keep refrigerated for up to 4 weeks.

To make the cocktail: place the ice sphere into a stemless wine glass. Place the remaining ingredients into a cocktail shaker, then shake with cubed ice and strain into the glass. Garnish with gold flakes and bee pollen.

COFFEE The coffee plays a supporting role to the other flavours, so any strong cold brew will work just fine. I tend to freeze cold brew that may be getting a little old into ice cubes to preserve it for drink occasions like this.

LIQUOR Cachaça of your choice is paired with this classic cherry liqueur.

CLASH OF STAGS

This cocktail was inspired by my desire to create a masculine interpretation of the Espresso Martini for those wanting a heavier hit of coffee and liquor, served in a more robust glass. It brings together two unlikely liquid personalities, both of which use a mighty stag in their logo. With the stags in mind, I conjured up visions of a hunt in the woods followed by cocktails beside a campfire. Substituting vodka for the big malt character of Glenfiddich whisky and the coffee liquor for the spiced bitter sweetness of Jägermeister, alongside a big dose of strong cold brew coffee to replace espresso, it delivers a powerhouse of flavours. When poured into a chilled rocks glass over cola, it creates a thick foam and aromatic effervescence, which bursts through the dusted surface.

15 ml/½ oz cola

35 ml/1¼ oz Glenfiddich 12 Years Old

22.5 ml/¾ oz Jägermeister

7.5 ml/¼ oz Vana Tallinn liqueur

45 ml/1½ oz cold brew coffee

1 star anise

3 cloves

1 orange zest (4 cm/1½ in)

To garnish
Cinnamon cocoa dust
1 star anise

Add the cola to a chilled rocks glass. Add the remaining ingredients to a cocktail shaker, fill with cubed ice and shake well. Strain into the glass over the cola. Garnish with the cinnamon cocoa dust and star anise.

COFFEE This drink is pretty versatile with regard to coffee due to the other robust flavours, so give it a go with whatever strong cold brew you have to hand.

LIQUOR Jägermeister and malt whisky work wonderfully together with the cold brew. Vana Tallinn liqueur, a lovely citrus, vanilla, cinnamon, rum-based liqueur from Estonia, is not essential to the recipe, but does pair really well with the other ingredients. If unavailable, it can be substituted with Cointreau.

FORBIDDEN FRUIT

This fruity offering is my interpretation of a drink designed by Canadian bartender Nanna Coppertone for a World Class UAE challenge. His design really impressed me, as he identified a subtle acidity in his coffee and matched that with the acidity of green apple. This works exceptionally well with the full agave character of the chosen Tequila, and the result is a is super-refreshing drink that is clean on the palate, which is often not the case with coffee cocktails.

45 ml/1½ oz Don Julio Blanco tequila

15 ml/½ oz Calvados apple brandy

30 ml/1 oz house espresso

15 ml/½ oz green apple and raisin shrub (see below)

To garnish

Malic acid, honey and popping candy

Granny Smith apple slice sprinkled with brown sugar and a pinch of cinnamon dust and caramelized using a blowtorch

Green apple and raisin shrub

400 ml/13½ oz freshly pressed Granny Smith apple juice

80 g/2¾ oz Sun-Maid raisins

30 ml/1 oz apple cider vinegar

15 ml/½ oz lime juice

200 g/1 cup caster/superfine sugar

For the green apple and raisin shrub: combine the ingredients in a sterilized jar. Press the raisins with a muddler, then stir, seal and allow to sit until the sugar is dissolved. Strain through a superbag (see page 42) into a bottle and keep refrigerated for up to 4 weeks.

To prepare the stemmed glass, coat the rim with malic acid, honey and popping candy, and fill with crushed ice.

To make the cocktail: add the ingredients to a cocktail shake, shake with cubed ice and double strain into a chilled stemmed glass. Garnish with the prepared apple slice.

COFFEE Your favourite house espresso.

LIQUOR I'm staying true to Nanna's drink by using Don Julio Blanco tequila. It has a vibrant, crisp apple freshness that pairs extremely well with both the shrub and coffee.

A BONNIE WEE FLIP

This drink is my interpretation of a Christmas Egg Nog. The Speyside whisky and Christmas mince pie mix makes such a stunning flavour pairing and the PX sherry ties everything together with its rich spice notes and added sweetness. I always use organic, free-range eggs and rinse them well before cracking them open. Make sure they're thoroughly whisked together so you get an even amount of yolk and white. For those unfamiliar with English Christmas mince pies, they do not contain minced meat – the name refers to minced stewed fruit and spices, including raisins, orange zest, cinnamon and cloves.

45 ml/1½ oz Christmas mince
   pie-spiced whisky (see below)
30 ml/1 oz cold brew coffee
15 ml/½ oz Pedro Ximénez sherry
30 ml/1 oz whisked egg white
   and yolk
7.5 ml/¼ oz Lyle's Golden Syrup

To garnish
Toasted and crushed almonds
Cinnamon powder

Christmas mince pie-spiced whisky
700 ml/23½ oz Speyside single
   malt whisky
200 g/6¾ oz Christmas mince
   pie filling

For the Christmas mince pie-spiced whisky: add the mince pie filling to the whisky and stir well to begin the infusion. Vacuum seal and sous-vide (see page 205) for an hour at 55°C/130°F. Remove, allow to cool and then strain into a bottle using a superbag (see page 42). The strained remains can be used to make boozy Christmas mince pies.

To make the cocktail: add the ingredients to a cocktail shaker, shake with cubed ice and double strain into a chilled Glencairn glass. Garnish with crushed almonds and cinnamon powder.

🫘 **COFFEE** A medium-bodied cold brew with notes of dried fruits works best.

🍾 **LIQUOR** I like to use a full-flavoured Speyside single malt like Glenfiddich 12 year or Singleton of Dufftown 12 year.

CRÈMA DE LA CRÈME

This is one of the drinks that inspired me to write this book. With such a great taste and presentation, I felt that it, along with many of my other coffee cocktails, needed to be shared with the world in the hope of inspiring others to get more creative with their cocktail designs. A velvety smooth, rich and punchy combination matches rum and blackberry with Guatemalan coffee, toasted chia seeds, a blend of bitters and cacao.

45 ml/1½ oz Ron Zacapa 23 rum
10 ml/⅓ oz Dark Crème de Cacao
35 ml/1¼ oz cold brew coffee
20 ml/⅔ oz toasted chia seed and blackberry syrup (see below)
Dash chocolate bitters
Dash aromatic bitters

To garnish
Blackberries
Dark chocolate flakes
Edible gold flakes
Mixed spiced powder (see below)

Toasted chia seed and blackberry syrup
50 g/1¾ oz chia seeds
250 g/1¼ cup white sugar
400 g/14 oz blended blackberries (approx. 2 punnets)

Mixed spiced powder
1 part ground vanilla bean
1 part ground cinnamon
¼ part ground ginger
¼ part ground nutmeg

For the toasted chia seed and blackberry syrup: crush the chia seeds and lightly toast in a hot pan. Add the white sugar and 250 ml/8½ oz water and bring to the boil. Add the blended blackberries and stir. Bring to the boil, then simmer for 12 minutes. Fine strain, allow to cool, then add to a sterilized glass bottle and refrigerate for up to 3 weeks.

For the mixed spice powder: combine the ingredients and mix well.

To make the cocktail: place a large ice block in an Old Fashioned glass. Add all the ingredients to a cocktail shaker, fill with cubed ice, then shake hard and double strain into the glass. Garnish.

COFFEE A full-bodied deep chocolatey cold brew works best here. The Guatemalan Arabica roast I used was a perfect match and links in with my preferred rum.

LIQUOR Ron Zacapa 23 is the star of the show, with its deep, rich, complex flavours gained from the Solera ageing process it goes through.

PEANUT BUTTER IRISH

A well-made Irish coffee is one of my favourite cocktails when consumed in the right place at the right time. Sadly that isn't too often when you live in the searing heat of Dubai, which is why I created a chilled version to enjoy on a hot day. To take it one step further, I first washed the Irish whiskey with peanut butter to add a rich nutty creaminess to the drink.

60 ml/2 oz peanut butter-washed Irish whiskey (see below)

90 ml/3 oz cold brew coffee

15 ml/½ oz soft brown sugar syrup 2:1 (see page 55)

90 ml/3 oz Baileys cream (see below)

To garnish
Light dusting of cinnamon powder
Coffee beans

Peanut butter-washed Irish whiskey
150 g/5⅓ oz raw unsalted 100 per cent peanut butter
1 litre/33 oz Irish whiskey

Baileys cream
(makes 4 servings)
60 ml/2 oz Baileys Irish Cream
310 ml/10½ oz whipping cream

Combine the peanut butter and the whiskey in a large vacuum bag and seal. Sous-vide (see page 205) at 55°C/130°F for 3 hours. Allow to cool then open the bag and run through a fine mesh strainer into a large jar and put in the freezer. Rest until the oils have frozen then strain through a fine muslin cloth to remove the remaining oils, then bottle and label. A little oiliness is fine as it will work in with the cream of the drink, but if you find there's too much you can re-strain, re-freeze and then put it through a paper coffee filter.

For the Baileys cream: add the Baileys to the whipping cream, shake and store in the refrigerator until ready to use.

To make the cocktail: add the ingredients, except the Baileys cream, to a cocktail shaker, shake and strain into a chilled rocks glass. Float with the Baileys cream. Garnish.

COFFEE A chocolatey Colombian, Guatemalan or Brazilian coffee works well with the whiskey. Either use a lower ratio brew such as 7:1 (see pages 40–43) or simply use 60 ml/2 oz at full strength and add 30 ml/1 oz water to dilute.

LIQUOR Choose your favourite entry-level Irish whiskey.

CAFFEINE CARNIVAL

Making and enjoying cocktails is all about having a good time, so sometimes you need to toss aside the classic rules and simply have fun! This whimsical creation is designed to make you feel like a kid again, and you get to both drink and eat it. The drink is served inside a cinnamon cronut cone, which has been sealed on the inside with a coating of dark chocolate. This extends to the rim, which is then dipped in sprinkles. Filled with an indulgent adult blend of vanilla vodka and Baileys Irish Cream, espresso and milk, it is impossible to resist!

Cinnamon cronut cone
Dark chocolate, melted
Candy sprinkles
45 ml/1½ oz vanilla vodka
15 ml/½ oz Baileys Irish Cream
30 ml/1 oz espresso
80 ml/2¾ oz full-cream milk

To garnish
Grated vanilla bean

To prepare the cronut cone: pour in the melted dark chocolate and allow it to cool to create a watertight seal around the inside, and dipping the rim into candy sprinkles.

To make the cocktail: put the remaining ingredients into a cocktail shaker, shake and strain the drink ingredients into the cone. Garnish with the vanilla bean.

COFFEE Standard espresso or cold brew both work fine for this cocktail, although the espresso's bitterness does help to balance the sugar of the cone.

LIQUOR Any vanilla vodka will do the trick.

PERUVIAN SOUR

At first thought coffee and lemon should clash, but in fact coffee's acidity can make a lovely pairing with lemon when balanced correctly. This recipe takes inspiration from Peru's hard-working coffee farmers by adding both coffee and Chicha Morada to Peru's national drink, the classic Pisco Sour. Chicha Morada is a traditional Peruvian beverage made by boiling purple corn with pineapple, cinnamon, cloves and sugar.

60 ml/2 oz Pisco
22.5 ml/¾ oz Chicha Morada coffee syrup (see below)
30 ml/1 oz fresh lemon juice
20 ml/⅔ oz egg white or chick pea brine for a vegan version

To garnish
Coffee & vanilla bitters mist

Chicha Morada coffee syrup
1 litre/33 oz Peruvian Chemex brewed coffee
1 litre/33 oz water
500 g/17 oz dried purple corn
Pineapple skin and core of 2 ripe pineapples
4 cinnamon sticks
½ tbsp cloves
1 diced Granny Smith apple
200g/1 cup granulated sugar

For the Chicha Morada coffee syrup: put the ingredients in a saucepan, bring to boil then simmer for 45 minutes and strain into a sterilized bottle. Refrigerate for up to 2 weeks.

To make the cocktail: add the ingredients to a cocktail shaker, fill with cubed ice, then shake and double strain into a chilled glass. Garnish with the coffee and vanilla bitters mist.

COFFEE It just seems natural to use a Peruvian coffee here for such a patriotic group of ingredients.

LIQUOR Ideally use a Quebranta grape-based Peruvian Pisco, such as Caravedo, as its earthy, dried fruit and subtle bitter clove character works well with coffee, rather than a Moscatel grape-based Pisco, which tend to be too floral to work particularly well with coffee.

TIRAMISU GELATO

The classic Italian dessert is a great example of coffee and liquor working well together and has been a favourite for bartenders to re-imagine since the 1980s. A simple marriage of espresso, Baileys, coffee liqueur and brandy shaken and strained into a Martini glass and dusted in cocoa powder, it is essentially an out-take on a Brandy Alexander and makes a great after-dinner drink, sure to impress your guests. My version takes the concept a few steps further.

40 ml/1⅓ oz VS Cognac
30 ml/1 oz cold brew coffee
15 ml/½ oz Baileys Irish Cream
7.5 ml/¼ oz coffee liqueur
3 dashes cacao bitters
1 scoop Tiramisu ice-cream
   (see page 197)

To decorate the glass
Crème de Cacao liqueur
Cocoa powder

To serve
Lady finger biscuit/cookie
   (optional)

To prepare the glass: spray the exterior of a large coupette glass with Crème de Cacao liqueur then dust with cocoa powder.

To make the cocktail: place the scoop of Tiramisu ice cream into a large coupette glass. Put the remaining ingredients into a cocktail shaker, fill with cubed ice, then shake and double strain into the glass. Serve with a lady finger biscuit/cookie, if you like, and a spoon.

COFFEE Any full-flavoured chocolatey espresso works well for this drink.

LIQUOR Any VS Cognac or decent-quality brandy will pair well with Baileys, bitters and coffee.

2 HOT

Coffee naturally works well hot so why aren't there more warming cocktails being enjoyed than a typical Irish or Baileys coffee? Hot cocktails are so underrated. When made well, they are a thing of beauty, elevating mood and warming you from the inside out. The heat amplifies the flavour and aroma, giving a heightened drinking experience. But getting the temperature just right is essential. Overheating can overcook ingredients, scald the lips and flatten mouthfeel. Underheating can make the cocktail underwhelming, causing the flavour and aroma to fall flat and losing that lovely warming sensation as the drink tickles your tonsils.

Bartender's tips

• Always preheat your vessel with hot water while you prepare the drink.

• Explore creative ways to heat drinks besides just adding hot water – for example, using a pan on a gas burner, a hot loggerhead or a steam wand, or by blazing.

• IMPORTANT SAFETY NOTE: Please blaze responsibly! Practise throwing with cold water first. Begin with the two jugs together at shoulder height and, as you pour, lower the bottom jug to create a continuous stream of liquid. Once mastered, try it with boiling water. Once you are ready for fire, do it in an open area of the bar where you won't be knocked by other staff members and where if you spill flaming liquor nothing important will catch fire. Ensure the jugs aren't too cool and that you don't pour all the liquid out from either jug as this may cause the flames to extinguish prematurely. Be aware that strong airflow or air-conditioning can cause issues. Have a wet tea towel/dish towel to hand to smother any flames or to cool singed hands.

IRISH COFFEE

The Buena Vista Cafe in San Francisco is credited with introducing the Irish Coffee to the USA in 1952. Stanton Delaplane, a travel writer, is said to have tasted the drink while in transit at Shannon airport, Ireland. Back in the US, he worked with the Buena Vista Cafe to recreate it. With painstaking effort put into getting the cream to float cleanly on top, they soon realized that adding sugar was the key. Stanton helped to popularize the drink by mentioning it frequently in his travel column. The team at Buena Vista Cafe have developed a rather unique style towards helping them serve so many Irish Coffees each day to throngs of enthusiastic tourists, and claim to have served more than 30 million since its inception! Elsewhere the Irish Coffee has sat fairly inconspicuously for decades, but The Dead Rabbit Grog and Grocery in New York has helped put it back in the spotlight, with their precision techniques and own custom glass to create what many claim to be quite possibly the best Irish Coffee in the world!

1 sugar cube or 1 tsp
   white sugar
45 ml/1½ oz Irish Whiskey
150 ml/5 oz hot espresso coffee –
   Americano/long black
75 ml/2½ oz double/heavy cream

To garnish
Grated nutmeg (many will serve it
   without, but personally I prefer
   it with for the touch of complexity
   and aroma it adds)

Preheat a goblet glass. Build the ingredients in the glass, making sure the sugar has dissolved and been stirred into the coffee and whiskey before gently layering with good-quality cream that's been shaken to a thicker but still fluid consistency. Garnish with nutmeg, if using.

COFFEE Traditionally any old filter coffee or espresso will do, but naturally the better the quality used, the better the end result will taste.

LIQUOR The Buena Vista Cafe uses Tullamore Dew, which I really like, but it tends to work well with most quality Irish Whiskeys.

KENTUCKY COFFEE

My recipe for this warming coffee cocktail has morphed over the years. It's one of my all-time favourite go-to drinks and has proven to be a real crowd-pleaser at a number of bars I've worked in during the colder winter months. When I get the chance, I'll ask to jump behind the bar to mix a round myself as it's a simple drink using ingredients available in any good bar. It was often referred to as a hot Espresso Martini by guests in my bars, but it's actually a very simple twist on the Irish coffee that works better in my opinion.

40 ml/1⅓ oz Bourbon
10 ml/⅓ oz dark Crème de Cacao
35 ml/1¼ oz espresso
10 ml/⅓ oz maple syrup
Dash of cacao bitters
90 ml/3 oz butterscotch cream
  (see below)

To garnish
Piece of dark chocolate
Cinnamon powder

Butterscotch cream
(makes 3 servings)
270 ml/9 oz whipping cream
15 ml/½ oz butterscotch liqueur

For the butterscotch cream: put the cream in a squeezy bottle and add the butterscotch liqueur. Shake to thicken.

To prepare the glass: take a piece of dark chocolate and gently warm the back with the flame of a lighter, and then press it on to the side of the Martini glass and put aside.

To make the cocktail: add the remaining ingredients to a Boston glass and heat using a coffee machine's steam wand until just before it hits boiling point. Pour into the room-temperature Martini glass. Layer with the butterscotch cream and garnish with cinnamon.

COFFEE House espresso works fine.

LIQUOR My personal favourite is Bulleit Bourbon as it has a high rye content that delivers a spiced nuttiness and works extremely well with the maple, coffee and cacao.

GINGERNUT LATTE

I designed this cocktail for a friend so he could mix himself something warming and yummy using his Nespresso machine for quiet nights in at home. It can, of course, be made with a classic espresso machine and steam wand. I've recommended using oat milk as it matches really well with the ginger spice and whisky, but it can also work with whatever you happen to have in your refrigerator, be it almond, cashew, soy or dairy milk.

45 ml/1½ oz whisky
10 ml/⅓ oz golden syrup
120 ml/4 oz oat milk
½ tsp dried ginger powder
Dash of cinnamon powder
1 shot Nespresso coffee

To garnish
Gingernut cookie crumbs
  and gingernut cookies served
  on the side (optional)

Add all the ingredients except the coffee to a Nespresso Aeroccino milk frother and turn on the hot setting. While that's warming, extract your Nespresso shot and pour it into a coffee cup. I recommend using a wide-mouthed glass so you can dunk your cookies.

Once the milk has heated, pour it over the top of the coffee. Garnish with gingernut cookie crumbs, and serve with gingernut cookies on the side, if you wish.

COFFEE Use whatever Nespresso pod you have to hand, but my recommendation would be something light-bodied such as the Livanto or Capriccio. The friend I designed this drink for often uses the flavoured pods and occasionally even decaff varieties.

LIQUOR Blended Scotch whisky tends to work best for this drink.

GODFATHER AFFOGATO

Don Corleone himself would be proud of this sumptuous twist on the timeless Italian after-dinner indulgence. It's so incredibly delicious and easy to make that it should be a staple on the menu for dinner party entertainers everywhere.

1 scoop zabaglione gelato (Italian egg yolk and Marsala wine ice cream – this can be substituted for vanilla bean or similar alternatives)

30 ml/1 oz Johnnie Walker Gold Label Reserve whisky

15 ml/½ oz amaretto

30 ml/1 oz espresso

To garnish
Crumbled biscotti
Cinnamon powder

To prepare the glass: place the scoop of gelato in a brandy balloon or coffee glass.

To make the cocktail: add the remaining ingredients to a Nespresso Aeroccino milk frother, turn it on to the red setting to heat, and mix it or use a steam wand on an espresso machine. Pour it over the gelato. Garnish with biscotti and cinnamon powder.

COFFEE House espresso works fine. Decaffeinated varieties are acceptable for late-night sessions.

LIQUOR The Gold Label is smooth and sweet, which pairs exceptionally well with a good-quality amaretto.

B52 HOT SHOT

Hot Shots (Galliano, hot coffee and whipped cream) were a fairly popular shooter at ski resorts back in the 1990s. Naturally I had to develop my own recipe while working in Queenstown (a New Zealand ski town) in 2007. This version is basically a twisted fusion of the Hot Shot and the B52 – it's deliciously warming from the inside out.

15 ml/½ oz Baileys
10 ml/⅓ oz Grand Marnier
15 ml/½ oz fresh hot espresso
5 ml/barspoon VS Cognac

Pour the Baileys into the glass first, so you get a nice smooth finish. Layer with Grand Marnier and coffee, which will blend together, and finally top with Cognac.

COFFEE House espresso works fine. I generally only make two at a time, so I can split an espresso between them. I've also made them at house parties using French Press/cafetière or stove-top moka-pot extractions.

LIQUOR The addition of the Cognac boosts the flavour and strength. Gold rum and Bourbon also work well.

WHISKEY POUR OVER

Pour-over brewing methods such as V60 and Chemex gently extract the subtle flavour characteristics from the coffee, which is ideal for showcasing the nuances of single origin roasts. Although this isn't an ideal method to apply to cocktails, there are a variety of ways it can be used. The simple method below combines the character of V60 coffee with a spirit of choice – in this case, whiskey. When drinking V60 coffee on its own, I never tend to add sugar, but when a spirit is added I feel that both benefit from the addition of some form of sugar to work as bridge and round out a balanced mouthfeel. The result is a lovely warming complex brew of invigorating goodness. Note that pouring spirits through paper filters can strip away certain characters, so I avoid doing so where possible.

15 g/½ oz single origin coffee, freshly ground

90 ml/3 oz whiskey

22.5 ml/¾ oz maple syrup

250 ml/8½ oz hot water (95°C/203°F)

To garnish
1 flamed orange zest per glass

Boil a kettle and pour hot water over the filter into the jug below to rinse the paper and preheat the jug. Add a small amount to each glass to preheat them. Remove the water from the jug.

Add freshly ground coffee to the filter. Put the whiskey and syrup into the jug and position under the filter. Pour the water slowly and steadily in a circular motion and wait for it to all drip through. Empty the warm water from the glasses and then fill with the cocktail in the jug. Garnish with the orange zest.

COFFEE Experiment using your favourite single origin coffees and match them to your dark spirits of choice.

LIQUOR I love American whiskey paired with coffee so have explored many options. My go-to is Maker's 46.

DUTCH COFFEE

This simple yet fun play on an Irish Coffee uses Dutch flavours of aged genever, Speculaas cinnamon liqueur, Dutch-style cold drip coffee and nutmeg, an ingredient that was once upon a time valued higher than gold by the famous Dutch East India company.

45 ml/1½ oz aged genever
15 ml/½ oz Speculaas liqueur
60 ml/2 oz cold drip coffee
Dash of cacao bitters
Layer with 60 ml/2 oz butterscotch cream (see page 96)

To garnish
Grated dark chocolate and nutmeg
A stroopwafel

To prepare the glass: preheat a stemmed glass with hot water, placing the stroopwafel on top so it begins to soften from the steam.

To make the cocktail: add all the ingredients except the butterscotch cream to a Boston glass and heat using a coffee machine's steam wand, until just before boiling point.

To serve: Empty the water and pour in the cocktail. Layer with butterscotch cream and garnish with grated chocolate and nutmeg. Place the stroopwafel on top to continue softening, then dunk, sip and enjoy.

COFFEE I recommend using a medium brew with strong notes of malt, cereal and nuts. I use an Indonesian Bourbon variety.

LIQUOR The aged genever has strong notes of malt and earthy notes that work really well with coffee and spice. There are some stunning Speculaas liqueurs available in Holland; if you can't find one, substitute for cinnamon liqueur or syrup.

MEXICAN MOCHA

This twist on a classic Irish Coffee was inspired by a trip to Oaxaca in Mexico, the home of mezcal and a city that has some amazing traditional uses for chocolate. Oaxaca is famous for its mole (savoury sauces), the most famous of which is the mole negro incorporating cacao and spices. A little less well known, but equally amazing, product is Oaxaca's drinking chocolate (see photo, opposite). In the village markets, shops grind down roasted cacao and blend it with sugar and spices to create cubes that can be crushed, using a Oaxacan swizzle stick called a molinillo, and then mixed into hot or cold water or milk to make a spiced chocolate drink.

40 ml/1⅓ oz reposado tequila

5 ml/barspoon mezcal

15 ml/½ oz spiced coffee liqueur (see Liquor, below right)

5 ml/barspoon agave syrup

2 nuggets of Oaxacan Semi-Amargo almond and cinnamon spiced chocolate (or cocoa powder)

90 ml/3 oz boiling water

60 ml/3 oz vanilla cream (5 ml/ barspoon pure vanilla extract to 100 ml/3¼ oz cream)

To garnish
Shaved dark chocolate

To prepare the glass: preheat a stemmed coffee glass and a mixing glass with hot water, then remove the water from both glasses.

To make the cocktail: add all ingredients except the boiling water and vanilla cream to the mixing glass. Crush the chocolate with a molinillo and swizzle until the chocolate has dissolved. Add the hot water and give a quick swizzle before pouring into the pre-heated coffee glass. Layer with cream. Garnish with dark chocolate.

COFFEE The coffee liqueur is a homemade recipe (see pages 186–187) but uses 1800 Silver tequila as the base with the addition of vanilla, chilli/chili powder, agave syrup and single origin Mexican cold brew coffee. Alternatively, use a quality brand coffee liqueur, like Mr Black or Quick Brown Fox, and add your own spices.

LIQUOR Quality tequila and smoky artisinal mezcal are paramount. Ideally use a tequila with rich notes of vanilla and orange such as 1800 Reposado, and a smoky mezcal such as Del Maguey Vida or Marca Negra Espadin.

CAMPFIRE MOCHA

A fun fireside interpretation of hot chocolate, this is the actual campfire recipe I made at the end of a long day out in the woods. I tend to pre-batch two or more serves into a bottle as it's a great drink to share with a friend around a fire. Naturally it works well made in the comfort of your kitchen or bar on a coffee machine using the steam wand to heat and mix it, but I'm certain it tastes best with campfire smoke in your eyes and mosquito bites on your arms!

For 2 servings
400 ml/13½ oz hot milk.
90 ml/3 oz Canadian whisky
2 tbsp unsweetened dark chocolate
  powder or cocoa
30 ml/1 oz maple syrup
80 ml/2¾ oz cold brew coffee

To garnish/serve
Toasted giant marshmallow

Add all the ingredients to a bottle. Shake then pour into a saucepan over the fire (don't burn it!). Once heated, whisk with a fork and pour into camping mugs. Best served with a toasted giant marshmallow.

COFFEE I use cold brew as it's super-convenient to take camping in a hip flask, but it also works well with espresso or even a stovetop moka pot.

LIQUOR Crown Royal or Canadian Club are great options as they're not intense whiskies, so they settle in well with the coffee and chocolate.

TASTE OF ARABIA

The process of brewing coffee as we know it began around the 15th century in Yemen, in the south of the Arabian Gulf. The local Arabs found it energized them by day and helped them stay up late for prayer in the evenings. The process they created soon made its way north through the Middle East and is still used today. There are now many different styles available, but the Arabs traditionally drink it strong, bitter, unsweetened, unfiltered, spiked with cardamom and accompanied with sweet dried fruits, particularly dates. Living in Dubai I have fallen in love with the traditional, ritualistic style of coffee. Here I've used the traditional method, but added more layers using local flavours.

For 4 servings
200 ml/6¾ oz toasted pine nut-infused vodka (see below)
10 ml/⅓ oz arak
2 dashes The Bitter Truth Aromatic Bitters (clove heavy)
60 ml/2 oz date syrup
300 ml/10 oz Arabic coffee
4 cardamom pods, crushed
Arabic cream (see below)

Toasted pine nut-infused vodka
1 litre/33 oz vodka
200 g/7 oz crushed pine nuts, lightly toasted

Arabic cream
100 ml/3¼ oz whipping cream
2 drops orange blossom water
4 strands saffron

To serve
Dried fruits

For the toasted pine nut-infused vodka: add the pine nuts to the vodka and allow to infuse for 24 hours, then strain through a superbag (see page 42) or muslin cloth.

For the Arabic cream: infuse the cream for 2 hours with the orange blossom water and saffron.

To make the cocktail: add the first four ingredients to a dallah (Arabic coffee pot) and put it aside while you make the coffee.

For the coffee: put 360 ml/12 oz water in a pan and bring to a simmer over a gas flame. Add the crushed cardamom pods and 50 g/1¾ oz of finely ground dark roasted Yemen or Ethiopian Arabica. Stir and return to a medium flame. Remove as the boil hits the top, stir and repeat twice more, then settle for 1 minute before pouring (without using a strainer) into the dallah pot, retaining the sediment in the bottom of the pan.

Swirl vigorously to mix well then pour out small cups and layer with the cream. Serve accompanied with dried fruits.

🫘 **COFFEE** Dark roasted Yemen or Ethiopian Arabica.

🍾 **LIQUOR** Use a vodka of your choice for infusing with pine nuts. Arak is a traditional Middle Eastern spirit with flavours of aniseed.

IMPERIAL COFFEE

Putting the beautiful Royal Belgian Balance syphon to use creates a theatrical interactive experience for your guests, especially when performed at the table. It's not practical to execute in a busy bar, but in the right environment it makes for a special serve. With smooth and warming flavours, this is a great drink for a couple of friends to share on a cold winter night.

90 ml/3 oz aged rum
2 dried orange wheels
1 dried fig, cut into small pieces
1 dried pineapple chunk
1 fresh ginger slice
2.5-cm/1-inch piece of liquorice/licorice root
16 g/½ oz fresh ground coffee
210 ml/7 oz water
30 ml/1 oz honey syrup (2:1 mix)

To garnish
½ dried orange slice
Liquorice/licorice root stick

Put the rum, fruit, ginger, liquorice/licorice and coffee in the syphon glass. Put the water and honey syrup in the metal chamber.

Ignite the flame and wait for the honey water to boil and transfer over to the glass. Allow to bubble for 15 seconds, then extinguish the flame. All the liquid will transfer back into the metal chamber, leaving the fruit and spice sediment behind.

Pour into stemmed glasses. Garnish with a dried orange slice and liquorice/licorice root stick.

COFFEE Use a medium ground coffee, similar to that used for a Chemex brew. Anything that pairs well with orange flavours, such as a honey-processed Nicaraguan, will work well.

LIQUOR I like a medium-bodied gold rum such as Mount Gay Eclipse, Matusalem Clásico, Bacardi 8 or Ron Zacapa Ámbar.

CAFE BRULOT DIABOLIQUE ▮▮▮

Translating to 'Devilishly Burned Coffee', the Cafe Brulot, as it's generally referred to, is a traditional hot coffee served after dinner. It was invented at Antoine's Restaurant in New Orleans by Jules Alciatore, the son of the restaurant's founder, and is still served daily for the awe of their guests. It is a fairly spectacular show as the bartender serves it from a chafing dish, ignites it and pours the flaming liquid down a long spiral of orange peel spiked with cloves. This process caramelizes the oils in the peel and toasts the cloves, creating a magnificent aroma through the room and into the drinks. This is a fairly technical and somewhat dangerous drink to execute, so should ideally be left to the professionals. If you do try it, I recommend doing so in a safe area of a bar or kitchen with a soaked tea towel/dish towel at hand to extinguish any stray flames or to cool singed fingers.

200 ml/6¾ oz brandy

400 ml/13½ oz French Press/
cafetière coffee

125 ml/4¼ oz orange Curaçao

3 tsp sugar

1 strip lemon zest

1 cinnamon stick

1 whole orange peel spiral pierced
with 8–10 cloves

To garnish
Orange zest spiked with cloves

Add all the ingredients except the coffee and orange peel to a saucepan or chafing dish and begin to heat. Stir with a long-handled spoon to dissolve the sugar. When it's hot enough, it will ignite.

With the liquid still flaming, use a long-handled fork or forceps to dangle the orange peel over the drink. Scoop up flaming liquid with a ladle and pour it down the spiral five times to char the spices and caramelize the orange oils. Drop the orange peel into the drink.

Pour in the hot coffee, which will extinguish the flame. Ladle into small coffee cups or sturdy stemmed glasses. Garnish with orange zest spiked with cloves.

COFFEE A full-bodied French Press/cafetière or filter coffee brew works well.

LIQUOR Medium-quality brandy or cognac works best here. Try not to burn it for too long. Cointreau or Grand Marnier are good substitutes if you don't have orange Curaçao to hand.

MEXICAN BLAZER

The classic Blue Blazer was first advertised by the legendary Professor Jerry Thomas in the first ever cocktail book, *The Bartenders Guide*, in 1862. It was the first documentation of flair bartending. JT is pictured throwing a flaming cocktail between two metal tankards to entertain his guests. To be honest, the classic recipe isn't particularly delicious, but with a few tweaks it can be, and there are plenty of alternative flavours that can be used. Here it's made using Mexican flavours (and can become a hybrid by adding a small knob of butter or mascarpone to make it similar to a Hot Buttered Rum cocktail). The Blazer is an extremely tricky and somewhat dangerous drink to master (see safety note, below). However, when it is made correctly and safely it can be stunning to enjoy in cold weather.

60 ml/2 oz Kah Reposado Tequila
10 ml/⅓ oz Cointreau
20 ml/⅔ oz boiling water
10 ml/⅓ oz agave nectar
30 ml/1 oz espresso
Dash of Black Walnut Bitters
Pinch of spice powder

To garnish
Orange zest
Cinnamon stick

IMPORTANT SAFETY NOTE
Please read the safety advice on page 93 before attempting to make this cocktail.

Preheat two metal milk jugs and a stemmed glass with hot water. Remove the water from jug one and add the tequila and Cointreau. Remove all but 20 ml/⅔ oz boiling water from jug two and add the agave, espresso and bitters.

Heat jug one with a blowtorch until the liquor is ignited and burning well. Slowly pour approximately 80 per cent of this flaming liquid in a continuous stream into jug two. Then pour 90 per cent from jug two back into jug one and repeat the process twice, finishing by pouring all of the liquid into one jug on the final pass.

Add a dash of spice powder, then extinguish the flame by placing the base of the empty jug on top of the other.

Empty the water from the glass and pour in the cocktail. Garnish with orange zest and a cinnamon stick.

🫘 **COFFEE** House espresso works fine.

🍾 **LIQUOR** The Kah tequila is high proof at 52% abv, which helps ignition and also has the body to handle being toned down a little. Cointreau is a perfect accompaniment. This recipe also works well with high-proof Bourbon and maple syrup, or with rum and golden syrup.

3 BUILT

These drinks are built in the glass one step at a time and then often require a stir or swizzle to bring the ingredients together. When building coffee drinks, you can often achieve beautiful presentation as the contrasting layers collide.

Bartender's tips

• When building a cold drink, ensure the coffee is room temperature or cooler so it doesn't melt your ice and over-dilute your drink.

• If you need to hold the glass, just use your finger and thumb on the base to avoid transferring unwanted warmth and oils on to the glass.

• Chill or heat your glass while you collect your ingredients together.

• When layering ingredients, the heavier/sweeter ingredients form the base and the lighter, higher abv ingredients sit on top.

• To swizzle a cocktail, use your barspoon or swizzle stick and roll it back and forth between your fingertips to agitate and mix well. This also creates extra dilution, which you may not achieve from a gentle stir.

BLACK/WHITE RUSSIAN

I've joined these two drinks together due to their similar and simple ingredients and construction. Essentially the White Russian is a twist on the original Black Russian. Both are named after their appearance and the fact that vodka is generally associated with Russia, particularly Stolichnaya and Smirnoff. The Black Russian, dating back to 1949, is credited to Belgian bartender Gustave Tops, who created it at the Hotel Metropole in Brussels by simply adding coffee liqueur to vodka over ice. Nowadays, many people request a cola top, which is an easy addition but creates an overly sweet adaptation. When, where and by whom the White Russian was created is unknown. It first appeared in print in an advertisement in the *Boston Globe* newspaper on the 21 March 1965 to promote a coffee liqueur (which is now no more) called 'Coffee Southern'. Proving a popular favourite in the '70s and '80s, it made a quick come back in 1998 after featuring as the favourite drink of Jeff Bridges' character, The Dude, in the movie *The Big Lebowski*. Simply a Black Russian topped with milk or often half milk/half cream, many prefer to shake a White Russian to combine the ingredients, but I feel the simple build is one of its charms. I also enjoy the aesthetic of pouring the milk over the top to create that lovely contrasting layer effect.

40 ml/1⅓ oz vodka
20 ml/⅔ oz coffee liqueur
45 ml/1½ oz cream/milk

To garnish
Nutmeg (optional)

Fill a rocks glass with cubed ice. Build the ingredients over the ice and stir. Garnish with nutmeg, if you like.

🫘 **COFFEE** Coffee liqueurs such as Kahlúa and Tia Maria work fine, but there are some stunning high-quality brands now available, such as Mr Black and Quick Brown Fox. Alternatively, you can make your own (see Chapter 6).

🍾 **LIQUOR** Select your favourite good-quality vodka.

COFFEE & TONIC

Bursting on to the scene in 2016 to much scepticism, the Coffee & Tonic has been a beverage revelation to many. Flavours you just wouldn't believe will work, do. Using coffee extracted by a cold brew or cold drip method produces a lot less bitterness than espresso. The tonic steps in and delivers this bitterness, plus the effervescence lifts the flavours to new heights and, hey presto, an elegantly refreshing summer cooler.

45 ml/1½ oz Tanqueray 10 gin
60 ml/2 oz cold brew coffee
120 ml/4 oz premium tonic water

To garnish
Grapefruit zest

Fill a highball glass with ice cubes. Build the ingredients over the ice and stir. Garnish with grapefruit zest.

COFFEE My cold brew preference is a light, complex Ethiopian, but of course feel free to experiment with your favourite roast.

LIQUOR Tanqueray 10 gin is a very citrus-forward gin using fresh orange, lime, grapefruit and chamomile in its construction, meaning it pairs very well with tonic and balances exceptionally well with complex coffees.

CAFE COCO

This extremely easy yet highly delicious twist on the White Russian simply switches out the dairy milk for a blend of coconut milk and coconut cream, and uses a quality cold brew coffee instead of a coffee liqueur. A touch of agave nectar adds sweetness. I often make these at home and have lost count of how many I consumed while writing this book!

45 ml/1½ oz vodka
60 ml/2 oz cold brew coffee
10 ml/⅓ oz agave nectar
45 ml/1½ oz coconut half & half
(see below)

To garnish
Toasted coconut flakes
Pinch of allspice

Coconut half & half
400 ml/14 oz can coconut cream
400 ml/14 oz can coconut milk

For the coconut half & half: mix a can of coconut cream with a can of coconut milk, bottle and refrigerate. Canned coconut has a long shelf life, so I do this regularly and use it as an addition to espresso shots and on my cereal.

To make the cocktail: fill the glass with ice. Build the ingredients over the ice and stir. Garnish with the coconut flakes and a pinch of allspice.

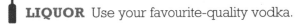

COFFEE My cold brew preference is a chocolatey Brazilian or Mexican.

LIQUOR Use your favourite-quality vodka.

CAFE L'ORANGE

This simple coffee cooler brings a lot of excitement to a regular cold brew routine and has now become my summertime Sunday afternoon go-to drink!

35 ml/1¼ oz VS Cognac
5 ml/barspoon Bénédictine liqueur
60 ml/2 oz cold brew coffee
5 ml/barspoon honey syrup
Dash of orange bitters
2 orange wedges

To garnish
Orange wheel
A cinnamon stick

Place crushed ice in a highball glass. Build the ingredients over the ice and swizzle to blend. Garnish with an orange wheel and cinnamon stick.

COFFEE Go nuts with your favourite cold brew or cold drip here – you can't go wrong!

LIQUOR VS Cognac is good quality and comes at a more affordable price than VSOP or XO, but has plenty of power to stand up and shine with the coffee and orange. The Bénédictine adds a little herbal complexity, but isn't essential if you don't have it stocked.

CAFE BALLER

I created this as an easy way to spice up a drink at home. By pre-making the coffee-spiced ice ball, I simply have to add it to my spirit of choice. It becomes more and more enjoyable as it slowly dissolves into the drink, lowering its temperature, and adding delicious coffee flavour and spices.

60 ml/2 oz spirit
Coffee-spiced ice ball
  (see page 188)

To garnish
Orange zest

Add 60 ml/2 oz of any spirit you love to a brandy balloon glass, add a pre-prepared coffee-spiced ice ball and garnish with orange zest.

COFFEE Make the ice ball with your favourite cold brew or cold drip coffee and spice it with vanilla, cinnamon, etc.

LIQUOR Premium Cognac, rum, tequila, whisky or whiskey all pair really well with the spiced ice. Liqueurs such as Cointreau, Grand Marnier, Drambuie, Glayva, Cherry Heering and many more also pair well as a sweeter treat.

COFFEE BOURBON FLOAT

Ice-cream and soda pop floats ought to bring a flood of fun childhood memories to even the most serious Martini imbibers and calorie counters. Laced with coffee and liquor, there's even more reason to treat yourself and bring a big smile to your face. Floats are seriously easy to twist into your own signature belt-busters, too, by adding different liquors and using sodas such as Dr Pepper, ginger beer or even a homemade spiced coffee soda (see page 189).

45 ml/1½ oz Bourbon
45 ml/1½ oz cold brew coffee
15 ml/½ oz dark crème de cacao
15 ml/½ oz maple syrup
2 dashes Fee Brothers Black Walnut
  Bitters
1 large scoop maple walnut
  ice-cream
60 ml/2 oz cola

To garnish
Pecans or walnuts
Cinnamon

Build the first five ingredients in a beer glass and stir, carefully drop in the ice-cream and top with cola. Garnish with pecans or walnuts and cinnamon.

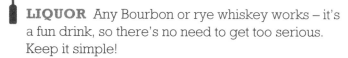

COFFEE Ideally you need a full-bodied, non-acidic dark roast cold brew.

LIQUOR Any Bourbon or rye whiskey works – it's a fun drink, so there's no need to get too serious. Keep it simple!

CINNAMON TOAST CRUNCH WHITE RUSSIAN

It's super-easy to add a touch of fun to a classic White Russian by simply infusing the half & half part with your favourite cereal. The cinnamon cereal not only adds a lovely sweetness, but also gives it a wholegrain wheat character.

30 ml/1 oz vanilla vodka

30 ml/1 oz coffee liqueur

90 ml/3 oz cereal-infused half & half (see below)

To garnish

Curiously Cinnamon/Cinnamon Toast Crunch cereal

Cereal-infused half & half

60 ml/2 oz milk

60 ml/2 oz cream

100g/3¼ oz Curiously Cinnamon/ Cinnamon Toast Crunch cereal

For the cereal-infused half & half: combine the milk and cream and add the cereal. Stir and leave to infuse for 15 minutes. Strain to remove the cereal.

To make the cocktail: fill a rocks glass with cubed ice. Build the ingredients, stir and garnish with cereal.

COFFEE Use a coffee liqueur of your choice or 30 ml/1 oz cold brew and 15 ml/½ oz sugar syrup (see page 55).

LIQUOR I used a homemade vanilla vodka, but feel free to use your favourite brand.

TENNESSEE JULEP

This drink was inspired by a visit to the George Dickel distillery in Tennessee. I was pleasantly surprised to discover this amazing American whisky is crafted in small batches in a very traditional manner using vintage equipment and processes that have stood the test of time. The quality of their product is heavily under-appreciated in the wider whiskey market, but I got the feeling they weren't too worried about trying to compete with the big boys down the road. They are content just making as much good whisky (they don't use the 'e') as they can at their own pace. That whisky happens to pair really well with coffee, so here's just one of many recipes I've played with since that visit.

60 ml/2 oz coffee-infused George Dickel No.8 Tennessee Whisky
5 ml/barspoon apricot liqueur
10 ml/⅓ oz light organic corn syrup
12 chocolate mint leaves

To garnish
5 mint sprigs
Half a canned apricot
A chunk of honeycomb

Add the ingredients to a Julep cup and swizzle with crushed ice to infuse the mint and dilute the syrup. Garnish with the mint, apricot and honeycomb.

COFFEE The coffee is infused directly into the whisky using the nitro-cavitation method (see page 196) to add a subtle touch of coffee.

LIQUOR George Dickel Tennessee Whisky uses the tradition of filtering the whisky through charcoal after distillation to refine its character. With hints of smoke, maple and buttered corn, it makes for a smooth and somewhat dry finish that pairs exceptionally well with coffee.

CAFE CORONA

No, this drink doesn't have beer in it! It was inspired by a cocktail called the Batanga and the man who makes it. Created by legendary bartender Don Javier Delgado Corona at his bar La Capilla, in the small town of Tequila in Mexico, it's basically a tequila and cola with fresh lime and a salt rim. Corona famously stirs it with a huge kitchen knife, which is used to cut the limes. Here I've replaced the cola with a variety of components, including spiced coffee soda, to give similar but different flavours.

45 ml/1½ oz 1800 Reposado
    Tequila
10 ml/⅓ oz Pierre Ferrand orange
    Curaçao
5 ml/barspoon mezcal
Spiced coffee soda (see page 189)
Dash of Bitter Truth Jerry Thomas
    Bitters

To garnish
Cocoa chilli/chili salt (see below)
Flamed orange zest

Cocoa chilli/chili salt
⅛ tsp cocoa powder
⅛ tsp chilli/chili powder
1 tsp Maldon sea salt

For the cocoa chilli salt: combine the cocoa powder, chilli/chili powder and sea salt.

To prepare the glass: rim a glass with the cocoa chilli/chili salt, then add ice.

To make the cocktail: build the ingredients and stir with a knife. Garnish with the orange zest.

COFFEE The coffee is whatever you've used to make the coffee soda, but with a touch of vanilla and toasted almond.

LIQUOR I'm a big fan of the 1800 tequila range for its rich body and flavour and it works so well here combined with coffee spices. Pierre Ferrand makes the best orange Curaçao on the planet; and the mezcal should be something smoky like a Del Maguey Vida or Marca Negra Espadin.

KEG PARTY

Nitro cold brew coffee became a hot trend in 2017. Coffee enthusiasts began hunting it down in their favourite specialty coffee shops and now even corporate coffee chains have jumped on the bandwagon. Nitrogen gas aerates the coffee and creates that sexy cascade effect we normally associate with Guinness. You're then left with a layer of that same lovely foam you get on the top of an Espresso Martini, which gives great mouthfeel. Bars have since started adding them to their menus by pre-mixing their recipes into refillable kegs and serving Nitro Cold Brew Martinis on tap. Not only do these offer great texture and deliciousness, but also speed and consistency. This basic recipe is super-easy to twist by changing up the sugar element to any number of flavours from salted caramel to guava or wherever your imagination may take you. This formula also works to serve from an iSi cream syphon if you don't have access to the mini keg system. The kit used is specialist but comes with detailed instructions. You will need 2 x 8 g nitrous oxide cartridges.

For 15 servings
300 ml/10 oz Ketel 1 Oranje vodka
600 ml/20 oz cold brew coffee 5:1 ratio (see pages 40–43)
200 ml/6¾ oz mineral water
150 ml/5 oz blackberry liqueur
50 ml/1¾ oz Pimento Dram
200 ml/6¾ oz agave syrup

To garnish
Chocolate powder (I spike mine with edible copper dust)
Blackberries

Add the ingredients to a pre-chilled 2 litre/66 oz keg, seal, shake, turn upside down and charge with 1 x No. 2 cartridge. Shake again and then charge with the second cartridge.

Pour into a chilled rocks glass with no ice. Sit the keg unit in an ice bucket filled with crushed ice to keep it nice and cold for your remaining serves.

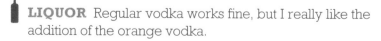

COFFEE My preference is to use a Colombian or Guatemalan with rich cacao flavours.

LIQUOR Regular vodka works fine, but I really like the addition of the orange vodka.

DEATH BY CAFFEINE

Designed as a dessert cocktail for a bar I used to manage that specialized in balls – meatballs, that is – this seemed like an appropriate cocktail to add to the menu. It was a fun and engaging experience for guests and when we sold one we'd end up selling half a dozen or more to curious onlookers wanting to experience it for themselves.

30 ml/1 oz Ron Zacapa Solera 23 rum
30 ml/1 oz cold brew coffee
15 ml/½ oz cinnamon-infused coffee liqueur
15 ml/½ oz Mayan spiced Amaro (see below)
15 ml/½ oz mineral water
2 dashes Dr. Adam Elmegirab's Aphrodite Bitters
Another 30 ml/1 oz cold brew coffee
Dark chocolate sphere
45 ml/1½ oz coffee foam (see page 198)

To garnish
Pop rocks
Freeze dried raspberry powder
Edible copper dust

Mayan spiced Amaro
700 ml/23½ oz Amaro Montenegro
5 ml/barspoon vanilla bean powder
3g toasted crushed cocoa nibs
0.2 g cinnamon powder
0.1 g chilli/chili powder

Pre-batch the first six ingredients x14 in a 1.5 litre/50 oz bottle and store in the refrigerator.

When ready to serve, pour the other 30 ml/1 oz cold brew coffee into a small ramekin and sit a dark chocolate sphere on top. Lightly flick a flame over the sphere using a blowtorch to slightly soften, then sprinkle with pop rocks, freeze dried raspberry powder and edible copper dust.

Lightly shake the pre-batched ingredients, measure out 105 ml/3½ oz and funnel into the sphere through a small hole in the top (see picture opposite, top left). Inject with coffee foam using an iSi gun (see picture opposite, top right). Insert a straw into the sphere.

Add a nugget of dry ice to the cold brew in the ramekin (see picture opposite, bottom left) and cover with a cloche (see picture opposite, bottom right).

To serve: remove the cloche and instruct the guest to sip the drink through the straw until it's gone, then crack open the chocolate sphere using a spoon and eat the chocolate paired with the chilled cold brew underneath.

Note: The coffee must have stopped misting completely before the cocktail is consumed.

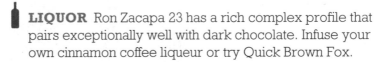

🫘 **COFFEE** Any cold brew that will match the chocolate sphere will work for both the cocktail and the shot.

🍾 **LIQUOR** Ron Zacapa 23 has a rich complex profile that pairs exceptionally well with dark chocolate. Infuse your own cinnamon coffee liqueur or try Quick Brown Fox.

4 STIRRED & THROWN

Stirring cocktails is a delicate, soothing ritual used to marry ingredients together to achieve precise dilution, while minimizing aeration and maximizing chill factor. The general rule of thumb is to stir liquor-heavy drinks that don't have too many thick heavy parts, such as syrups and juices (these ingredients may not combine effectively through such a gentle process). Stirring rather than shaking helps you to retain the clarity of drinks such as Manhattans, Martinis, Old Fashioneds and Negronis. In comparison to shaking, the drink won't quite reach the same temperature low and the amount of oxygen put through the ingredients is a lot less, which results in a very different viscosity and mouthfeel finish.

Throwing is used for similar drinks that need more mixing and aeration. It is now frequently seen in bars, but in fact pre-dates shaking – prior to fitting two metal tins together, drinks were thrown between them to combine the ingredients.

Bartender's tips – Stirred

• Stirred drinks should be served as cold as possible, so chill the glass and the mixing vessel first with ice. Stir the ice to create more ice to glass contact for faster chilling.

• Prepare your garnish while the glassware is chilling so it's ready to use.

• Pour away excess water that has melted while the mixing vessel was chilling.

• Use large cubes or cracked chunks of ice. Small ice will dilute too quickly and not chill enough, while large blocks will dilute and chill too slowly and require a lot of stirring.

• Once you begin pouring in the liquids, move purposefully as the dilution has begun.

• Ensure the ice sits above the liquid.

• Stir in a smooth but fluid movement; be gentle with the ice.

• Serve the drink as quickly as possible so it can be enjoyed at its peak.

Bartender's tips – Thrown

• Thrown drinks should be served as cold as possible, so always chill the glass with ice while preparing the drink.

• Add ice to the one tin containing your drink and fit it with a prongless strainer. Leave the other one empty.

• Find a fluid motion to pass the liquid from the iced tin to the empty one. Start high to one side and as you rotate drop your bottom hand. Pass the liquids back and repeat.

• Practice makes perfect so when starting out try with water to find your comfort zone.

COFFEE MARMALADE OLD FASHIONED

This drink takes the classic Old Fashioned cocktail formula and sends it into orbit with the addition of a caffeinated boost and the bittersweet brilliance of orange marmalade.

3 coffee beans

2 barspoons orange marmalade

3 dashes coffee bitters
  (see page 192)

1 dash chocolate bitters

7.5 ml/¼ oz soda water

60 ml/2 oz Johnnie Walker Black
  Label whisky

To garnish

Orange zest

Chocolate-coated coffee beans
  on the side, sprayed with orange
  zest oil

Crush the coffee beans in a chilled mixing glass, then add the marmalade, bitters and soda water and stir to dissolve the marmalade. Add cubed ice and whisky and stir until it reaches the correct dilution and temperature.

Double strain over ice in a chilled Old Fashioned glass. Garnish with orange zest.

COFFEE Go with your favourite medium-roasted fresh coffee beans – the bitters will back them up with an added layer of complexity.

LIQUOR This drink is versatile enough to work with a wide variety of whiskies and whiskeys, but I just love it with Black Label. The orange and coffee complement it so well.

CAFE MANHATTAN

I consider a perfectly balanced Manhattan to be one of life's true pleasures. The only thing that could possibly make it better is the influence of freshly ground coffee and maybe a cheeky slice of Tiramisu on the side.

50 ml/1¾ oz coffee-infused rye whiskey (see page 195)
20 ml/⅔ oz Mancino Rosso Amaranto vermouth
1 dash Black Walnut Bitters
2 dashes cherry bitters

To garnish
Flamed orange zest (discarded)
Cointreau & Cognac soaked cherry

Stir the ingredients over ice and strain into a chilled coupette glass. Garnish and serve.

COFFEE The coffee is infused into the whiskey to add a subtle character to complement the spiced nuttiness of the rye. I like a honey-washed Costa Rican.

LIQUOR Rye whiskey has a drier winter-spice character in comparison to Bourbon. This is balanced with the Mancino Rosso Amaranto vermouth, which has a lot of complexity and a rich sweetness.

CAFE NEGRONI

Negronis have had a huge rise in popularity over recent years due to their broad, complex flavour profile, ease of mixing and versatility. For those that like a little bitterness, they really do tick all the right boxes. This is one of my favourite drinks and the best part is its versatility; it can be adapted using your base spirit of choice.

25 ml/¾ oz Rutte Old Simon genever
22.5 ml/¾ oz coffee-infused sweet vermouth (see page 194)
22.5 ml/¾ oz Rinomato bitter aperitivo

To garnish
Flamed orange zest
Pomegranate molasses painted on the side of the glass (optional)

Place a large chunk of ice in a stemless wine glass. Add all the ingredients to a cocktail shaker with cubed ice and throw 5 times to mix, chill and gently aerate, then strain into the glass. Garnish.

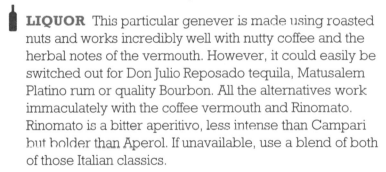

COFFEE The coffee is infused into the vermouth to add a subtle character and deepen its flavour.

LIQUOR This particular genever is made using roasted nuts and works incredibly well with nutty coffee and the herbal notes of the vermouth. However, it could easily be switched out for Don Julio Reposado tequila, Matusalem Platino rum or quality Bourbon. All the alternatives work immaculately with the coffee vermouth and Rinomato. Rinomato is a bitter aperitivo, less intense than Campari but bolder than Aperol. If unavailable, use a blend of both of those Italian classics.

SMOKY BOBBY BURNS

The Bobby Burns cocktail is an adaptation of a Manhattan, substituting Scotch whisky for American rye whiskey or bourbon and a touch of Bénédictine, which is a herbal liqueur produced by French monks, My version is enhanced with coffee and a sweet aromatic smoke. I have to say I'm not usually a huge fan of smoked cocktails as I've had so many made with woodchips that create an acrid burnt ashtray aroma. It's important to find chips that produce a delicious smoke that will enhance the drink and not just be used for the visual appeal. Also, don't blast the woodchips with too much heat as that can create a bitter smoke. When you get it right, it adds a lovely layer of complexity to your cocktails.

Lemon zest
40 ml/1⅓ oz Monkey Shoulder
  Scotch whisky
30 ml/1 oz coffee-infused vermouth
  (see page 194)
10 ml/⅓ oz Bénédictine liqueur

To serve
Scottish shortbread (optional)

Express the lemon oils into a chilled mixing tin and discard the zest. Add the other ingredients and throw between two tins with ice approximately 6 times.

Strain into a large chilled balloon glass with a narrow opening and smoke using a smoking gun with dried chocolate malted barley and American oak woodchips from an old cask.

Serve with some Scottish shortbread on the side, if you like. Instruct the drinker to swirl the drink vigorously before sipping to integrate the smoke and clear the majority of it out of the vessel before sipping.

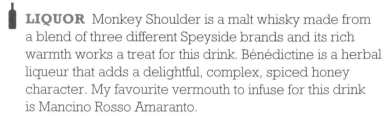

COFFEE The coffee is subtly delivered through the infusion into the vermouth.

LIQUOR Monkey Shoulder is a malt whisky made from a blend of three different Speyside brands and its rich warmth works a treat for this drink. Bénédictine is a herbal liqueur that adds a delightful, complex, spiced honey character. My favourite vermouth to infuse for this drink is Mancino Rosso Amaranto.

HANKY PANKY

This bitter-sweet Martini was first created by Ada Coleman at the legendary American Bar at the Savoy, London, where she began working as a bartender in 1903. It's a bold and often polarizing cocktail, not suited to all, but if you love a good Negroni, give this a crack. The subtle coffee adds an invigorating layer of complexity that works as a nice bridge for the Fernet-Branca.

30 ml/1 oz London Dry Gin
30 ml/1 oz coffee-infused sweet
  vermouth (see page 194)
2.5 ml Fernet-Branca

To garnish
Orange zest oils

Stir the ingredients over ice in a mixing glass and strain into a coupette glass over a small chunk of hand-cut ice.

Garnish with orange zest oils.

COFFEE The coffee is delivered through the infusion into the vermouth and pairs extremely well with the Fernet-Branca.

LIQUOR With the recent explosion on the market for gin, we are incredibly spoilt for choice. I tend to avoid anything too juniper-heavy and go for something citrusy or spiced/nutty. Tanqueray No 10 works exceptionally well to lighten this drink up, as does Bombay Sapphire or to follow the spice route try G'Vine Nouaison, Bombay Sapphire East or Tanqueray Malacca.

VIEUX CAFE

You guessed it, this is a coffee twist on that epic New Orleans' classic, the Vieux Carré, my favourite booze-heavy classic of all time. The split base of rye and Cognac delivers complex sweet and spice, which is rounded out and herbalized with the vermouth and then elevated with the blend of bitters, coffee and a touch of Bénédictine.

22.5 ml/¾ oz rye whiskey

22.5 ml/¾ oz Cognac VS

22.5 ml/¾ oz coffee-infused sweet vermouth (see page 194)

5 ml/barspoon Bénédictine liqueur

1 dash Peychaud's Bitters

1 dash Dr. Adam Elmegirab's Orinoco Bitters

To garnish
Flamed orange zest

Add the ingredients to a shaker with cubed ice and throw 5 times to mix, chill and gently aerate. Strain into a Martini glass with no ice. Garnish with flamed orange zest.

 **COFFEE** The coffee is infused into the vermouth to add a subtle character to deepen its complexity and flavour.

LIQUOR Use your favourite quality brands to create a complex balance of flavours.

BOTTLED CAFE ROSITA

Very similar to the Negroni recipe on page 151, this one swaps out the genever for Reposado tequila and is pre-bottled so it can be instantly served direct from the refrigerator. Salted dark chocolate (such as Terry's Dark Chocolate Orange) is a fun but not essential accompaniment.

25 ml/¾ oz Reposado tequila
22.5 ml/¾ oz coffee-infused sweet vermouth (see page 194)
22.5 ml/¾ oz Rinomato bitter aperitivo

To garnish
Flamed orange zest

Multiply the recipe ingredients to fit your bottle size, whether that be for 2 serves or 10+. Fill the bottle with the ingredients and store in the refrigerator.

To serve: simply prep glasses with ice and garnish, and place the bottle next to it for guests to pour and stir their own drink.

COFFEE The coffee is infused into the vermouth to add a subtle character to deepen its flavour.

LIQUOR My favourite tequilas for this drink are Fortaleza, Don Julio or Arette. However, you can choose your favourite quality Reposado ('rested') tequila to pair with the Rinomato (see page 151).

SAMMY DAVIS

I created this to honour the character, charisma and class of the Rat Pack legend and original Mr Bojangles, Mr Sammy Davis Jnr. It was a classic clip on YouTube of Sammy doing a Suntory whisky advert that inspired me to design a drink I'm certain he would have loved.

45 ml/1½ oz Suntory Kakubin Yellow Label blended whisky

20 ml/¾ oz Lustau Pedro Ximénez sherry vermouth

2 atomized sprays Octomore whisky

1 large block of cold brew coffee ice (see page 188)

To garnish

Spray of Octomore whisky from atomizer on to an open flame

Mini moka pot with cold brew and dry ice for an aromatic haze effect (optional)

Add the first three ingredients to a mixing glass and stir over ice.

Add the block of coffee ice and strain the cocktail over the top. Garnish.

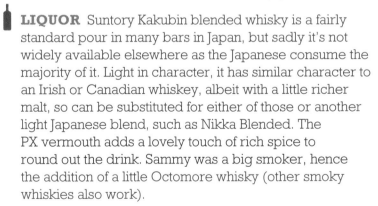

COFFEE The coffee is applied through cold brew ice so choose a brew that works with the whisky you use.

LIQUOR Suntory Kakubin blended whisky is a fairly standard pour in many bars in Japan, but sadly it's not widely available elsewhere as the Japanese consume the majority of it. Light in character, it has similar character to an Irish or Canadian whiskey, albeit with a little richer malt, so can be substituted for either of those or another light Japanese blend, such as Nikka Blended. The PX vermouth adds a lovely touch of rich spice to round out the drink. Sammy was a big smoker, hence the addition of a little Octomore whisky (other smoky whiskies also work).

OAK AGED OLD FASHIONED

This coffee-enhanced Old Fashioned is finished with a little time ageing in an oak bottle or barrel, which means that this serve requires a little thinking ahead, but it's well worth it for the result.

50 ml/1¾ oz Bourbon whiskey

7.5 ml/¼ oz sugar syrup (2:1 ratio)
(see page 55)

5 ml/barspoon coffee liqueur

10 ml/⅓ oz mineral water

3 dashes coffee bitters
(see page 192)

To garnish
Orange zest
Piece of Lindt orange chocolate
with sea salt

Multiply the recipe by the number of serves you wish to prepare to suit your ageing vessel. Build all the ingredients together in a large container. Stir well and taste to ensure the balance is correct; adjust if needed to suit your ingredients. Decant into a pre-seasoned (see note, below) oak vessel and leave to mature.

When ready to serve, simply pour 75 ml/2½ oz over a large chunk of ice in an Old Fashioned glass, and garnish.

Seasoning: this is the act of using a liquid in your oak vessel to impart flavours that will pass across to the next drink. While many things can work, here I suggest making a large but light French Press/cafetière coffee and then filling the oak vessel and leaving it to soak for 24–48 hours before removing.

Bartender's Tip: when ageing spirits in oak, think of it like adding an extra ingredient – too little and there is no point, too much and it will overwhelm the other flavours. So you need to taste the liquid regularly until you find that sweet spot, then you can remove it and store in glass to maintain the desired flavour.

Note: the smaller the vessel, the faster the drink will age. Also be aware that temperature, oak age and abv can all have an effect on timing, so this cocktail will have different timings to others.

🫘 **COFFEE** The liqueur, bitters and barrel seasoning all add easy-going coffee notes to complement the drink.

🍾 **LIQUOR** Go with the Bourbon of your choice. I've found Maker's Mark or Jim Beam Black Label both work really well. I'm sure the formula will also work great with many rums, Scotches and even Cognac.

TURKISH DELIGHT

This recipe was inspired by my Turkish friend, Mehmet Sur, who designed a similar drink to showcase at the 2015 World Class Global cocktail competition, held in South Africa. It celebrates Turkish flavours and their coffee culture, which is incredibly historic and intriguing.

30 ml/1 oz Turkish coffee
45 ml/1½ oz Ron Zacapa 23 rum
15 ml/½ oz Oloroso sherry
60 ml/2 oz Turkish Delight air
  (see below)

To serve (optional)
Assorted dried fruits
Pistachio nuts
Turkish Delight

Turkish Delight air
150 ml/5 oz boiling water
50 g/1¾ oz sultanas
50 g/1¾ oz dried hibiscus flowers
15 ml/½ oz Royal Jelly & Ginseng
  Honey (Yemen)
10 ml/⅓ oz raki
3 drops rose water
1 g Sucro aeration powder

For the Turkish Delight air: muddle the sultanas into boiling water, add the hibiscus flowers and allow to sit for 8–10 minutes before straining. Add the remaining ingredients and chill.

To make the cocktail: make the coffee fresh, then strain it into a chilled ibrik jug or shaker tin. Add the rum, sherry and cubed ice, then throw back and forth until optimum dilution is achieved. Strain into a chilled Turkish coffee glass or similar.

To serve: aerate the Turkish delight air with a stick blender or electric whisk and spoon on top of the drink. Serve accompanied with assorted dried fruits, pistachio nuts and Turkish Delight, if you like.

COFFEE Turkish coffee is dark roasted, very finely ground and the water is heated to a high temperature in an ibrik pot (the small wooden-handled jugs pictured). It's generally strong and bitter. You can substitute it for strong espresso.

LIQUOR Ron Zacapa 23 is a full-flavoured, complex, sweet rum that works as a solid base which integrates really well with all of the other flavours. Oloroso sherry has a lovely spiced nuttiness to it, and raki is a traditional Turkish spirit distilled from fermented grapes and flavoured with anise.

5 BLENDED

Once upon a time, blenders were a must-have in bars to create the colourful disco drinks of the late '70s and '80s. They slowly fell out of favour as the muddler became the bartender's new favourite toy. Most high-profile bars have banished their noisy, cumbersome, inconsistent blenders to dark cupboards back of house next to their spherification kits and manual credit card swiping machines, leaving them to Tiki-shirt-clad poolside bartenders to deal with. But a well-made blended drink really is a thing of beauty when the balance of quality ingredients is just right. Velvety smooth and cooling, they can take you away to your happy place. Blending quality cocktails is nowadays somewhat of a lost art that takes practice and precision to achieve great results. The key as with any cocktail is quality ingredients and far too often bartenders feel the need to load blended drinks up with sugary syrups and liqueurs. Keep it fresh, guys! Just as important is the correct ratio of ice. Too little and you have a lukewarm sloppy mess, but worse still and more common is too much ice! Besides an overly icy chunky texture, the main issue is that ice is water and water dilutes flavour! If there's anything left in the blender, too much ice has been used – that excess is flavour that should be in your drink and it means your glass has too much blended ice in it.

Bartender's tips

• For these blended drinks loaded with various other flavours you can be a little less fussy about the coffee you choose. Typically any strong cold brew or espresso will work fine within reason.

• Always blend with crushed or cracked ice.

• Too much ice will over-dilute the flavours and make the cocktail too solid and difficult to consume. It won't blend well and you'll more than likely be left with ice chunks in the glass. All this creates a disappointing experience that will often ruin peoples perception of blended drinks.

• Not enough ice will mean a sloppy drink that'll lose that super-frostiness we love from a well-blended drink.

• Peek in the top of the blender – you'll know the drink is ready when you can see a smooth tight whirlpool spinning in the centre.

F.B.I.

The Frozen Black Irish is technically a classic, although it has slipped off most people's radar since the noughties. There's very little info to be found on it, other than it was a TGI Friday's original dating back to circa 1985, and that it is quite likely related to the Frozen Irish Coffee and the Mudslide, a sweeter version that is doused in chocolate sauce and whipped cream. The F.B.I. is a super-simple and somewhat restrained drink compared to the plethora of colourful blended disco drinks that emerged in that '80s era. The original is pretty tasty, but it has the potential to be so much better with a few tweaks. I've enhanced it here with an extra kick of cold brew and good premium vanilla bean ice cream. Traditionally these are served with no garnish (naked), but here I've borrowed the idea of using coffee grinds as used to decorate the cult classic Frozen Irish coffee, which is served at Erin Rose in New Orleans from a frozen Daiquiri slushy machine.

30 ml/1 oz vodka

30 ml/1 oz Baileys Irish Cream

30 ml/1 oz Kahlúa coffee liqueur

30 ml/1 oz cold brew coffee

2 scoops vanilla bean ice-cream

45 ml/1½ oz half & half (see page 204)

½ scoop crushed ice

To garnish

Crushed instant coffee granules blended with dried vanilla bean dust

Blend the ingredients until smooth and frosty cold. Pour into an Old Fashioned glass. Garnish with the coffee granules.

🫘 **COFFEE** The original recipe calls for Kahlúa coffee liqueur, which does the trick, or step up your game with one of many new products on the market using high-quality ingredients such as Mr Black, Quick Brown Fox, Little Drippa, Black Twist or Bébo. My recipe uses a good-quality strong cold brew that delivers more depth of flavour than the original.

🍾 **LIQUOR** Any house vodka tends to work in the original. Irish whiskey also works really well as it boosts the character and brings the flavour to life.

FRAPPÉ ITALIANO

Hot afternoons spent exploring Italy inspired this frosty frappé twist on the Starbucks classic. Bittersweet and herbal, all three of the liquors used are Italian after-dinner icons. When blended with ice and boosted with cold brew coffee, they create an atomic Italian ice bomb.

30 ml/1 oz Marsala Superiore dolce fortified wine
20 ml/¾ oz Amaro Ramazzotti
10 ml/⅓ oz Fernet-Branca
45 ml/1½ oz cold brew coffee
10 ml/⅓ oz Amarena cherry syrup
1 scoop crushed ice

To garnish
Fresh mint
An Amarena cherry

Blend the ingredients until icy smooth and serve in a goblet glass or disposable coffee cup. Garnish with mint and an Amarena cherry.

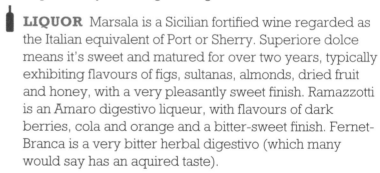

COFFEE Go nuts with your favourite cold brew or cold drip here – you can't go wrong!

LIQUOR Marsala is a Sicilian fortified wine regarded as the Italian equivalent of Port or Sherry. Superiore dolce means it's sweet and matured for over two years, typically exhibiting flavours of figs, sultanas, almonds, dried fruit and honey, with a very pleasantly sweet finish. Ramazzotti is an Amaro digestivo liqueur, with flavours of dark berries, cola and orange and a bitter-sweet finish. Fernet-Branca is a very bitter herbal digestivo (which many would say has an aquired taste).

POP IT LIKE IT'S HOT!

The name says it all! Actually super-easy to make, this one is fun to do as a treat for your friends.

40 ml/1⅓ oz Monkey Shoulder whisky
40 ml/1⅓ oz cold brew coffee
90 ml/3 oz milk
2 scoops vanilla ice cream
4 caramel popcorns
30 ml/1 oz caramel sauce
Pinch of salt

To garnish
Caramel sauce
Whipped vanilla cream
Caramel popcorn

Drizzle a milkshake glass with caramel sauce. Blend the ingredients with half a scoop of crushed ice and pour into the glass. Garnish with whipped vanilla cream, caramel popcorn and more caramel sauce, if desired.

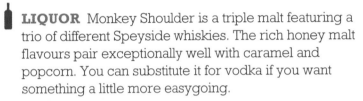

COFFEE You can't go wrong with any cold brew.

LIQUOR Monkey Shoulder is a triple malt featuring a trio of different Speyside whiskies. The rich honey malt flavours pair exceptionally well with caramel and popcorn. You can substitute it for vodka if you want something a little more easygoing.

NETFLIX 'N' CHILLED

This delicious but somewhat naughty creation was devised at home when I was tasked with making dessert for a session of Netflix 'n' chill. The ice-cream tub is a fun touch but optional. I simply used it rather than throwing it out after scraping the last remains into the blender, as a way of doing fewer dishes. This recipe is for two, but can be halved to fill a regular glass for one. This style of recipe can easily be adapted to suit other exotic ice-cream flavours, such as Macadamia Nut Brittle, Salted Caramel and Belgian Chocolate.

For 2 servings
90 ml/3 oz Bourbon
45 ml/1½ oz cold brew coffee
4 scoops cookie dough ice cream
120 ml/4 oz milk
60 ml/2 oz maple syrup
Pinch of salt

To garnish
Whipped cream
A cookie
Cookie crumbs

Blend the ingredients and pour into a large sharing glass or ice cream tub. Garnish.

COFFEE You can't go wrong with any cold brew. In fact, use whatever strong coffee you have to hand – espresso, Nespresso, Moka pot, etc.

LIQUOR I love Bourbon or Jack Daniels to pair with these flavours.

COFFEE ROCKY ROAD

Chocolate, coffee, raspberry and ice cream crowned with toasted marshmallows. Oops. Sorry, not sorry! I gave this to a friend once on their birthday with candles and a silly hat.

45 ml/1½ oz vodka
30 ml/1 oz cold brew coffee
15 ml/½ oz coffee liqueur
20 ml/⅔ oz raspberry purée
90 ml/3 oz milk
2 scoops vanilla ice cream
45 ml/1½ oz chocolate sauce
10 ml/⅓ oz vanilla syrup
Pinch of salt

To garnish
Chocolate sauce
Cookie crumbs
Blowtorch-toasted marshmallows
   with a dash of cinnamon tossed
   into the flames

To prepare the glass: rim a milkshake glass with the chocolate sauce and cookie crumbs.

To make the cocktail: blend the ingredients with half a scoop of crushed ice and pour into the glass. Top with marshmallows, toast with a blowtorch, and add a dash of cinnamon.

COFFEE Any cold brew or espresso works well for this recipe.

LIQUOR Any vodka of your choice works well – in fact, you could go wild with one of the funky flavours out there like birthday cake, chocolate cherry or cookie dough if you wish!

NEW YORK CAFE CREAM

The New York Egg Cream is a classic drink style said to have been invented in New York by a Jewish immigrant in the 1920s. Nowadays, it contains neither eggs nor cream, but strong arguments can be found supporting recipes both with and without in regards to the original. I prefer to use neither and instead pimp it with a few other luxuries.

45 ml/1½ oz Bourbon whiskey

20 ml/⅔ oz Mozart Dark Chocolate liqueur

90 ml/3 oz almond milk

30 ml/1 oz cold brew coffee

15 ml/½ oz toasted cacao syrup (see below) or chocolate fudge sauce

½ scoop crushed ice

45 ml/1½ oz soda

To garnish

Boozy chocolate ganache (see page 200)

Toasted cocoa nibs

Toasted cacao syrup

300 g/10½ oz crushed cacao nibs

500 g/2½ cups caster/superfine sugar

500 g/2½ cups coconut sugar

For the toasted cacao syrup: add the crushed cacao nibs to a pan and toast gently. When ready, add the caster/superfine sugar and coconut sugar and begin to soften. Add 1 litre/ 33 oz water, stir, bring to the boil then set to simmer. Stir well, until the sugar has dissolved, then allow to cool and strain before bottling.

To prepare the glass: dip the rim of a tall glass into boozy chocolate ganache. Sprinkle with toasted cocoa nibs.

To make the cocktail: blend all the ingredients, except the soda, until velvety smooth then pour into the glass. Top with soda and watch it foam.

COFFEE Any cold brew works well.

LIQUOR Bourbon with coffee and chocolate... drool. Any entry-level Bourbon works. I used Mozart Dark Chocolate liqueur, which is delicious, but if it's unavailable, Baileys Chocolat Luxe liqueur or other similar products will work just as well.

CAFE COLADA

This crafty twist on the Piña Colada has proven to be a big crowd-pleaser at numerous events. By switching out the pineapple for coffee and the coconut cream for coconut rum, and adding a touch of spice and crushed ice to the blender with premium rum, you get a smooth and rich experience without the often sickly creaminess of a traditional Colada. The edible coating on the glass adds a touch of fun.

45 ml/1½ oz Ron Zacapa 23 rum
45 ml/1½ oz cold brew coffee
15 ml/½ oz coconut rum
15 ml/½ oz Caribbean spiced syrup (see below)
¼ scoop crushed ice
2 dashes chocolate bitters

To garnish/coat the glass
Coconut liqueur
Shredded coconut
Vanilla bean dust
Cocoa powder

Caribbean spiced syrup
1 g allspice powder
1 g nutmeg powder
0.3 g ginger powder
1 litre/33 oz mineral water
1.8 kg/8 cups caster/superfine sugar
3 g pure vanilla extract
200 g/1 cup coconut sugar

For the Caribbean spiced syrup: add the spice powders to a pan and lightly toast. Add the water and bring to the boil, then add the caster/superfine sugar and vanilla extract. Simmer until dissolved. Run through a fine-mesh strainer to remove some of the powder, then add the coconut sugar and stir to dissolve. Allow to cool, pour into a sterilized bottle and store in the refrigerator for 8 weeks.

To prepare the glass: spray the exterior of a (preferably round) Old Fashioned glass with coconut liqueur from an atomizer bottle, then dust it with a coating of shredded coconut mixed with vanilla bean dust and cocoa powder. I like to get carried away and coat the whole glass when there's a handle to keep fingers clean.

To make the cocktail: blend the ingredients into a light smooth frosty liquid and pour into the pre-coated glass. Top with fresh shredded coconut.

COFFEE My favourite cold brew for this drink is a rich Guatemalan roast to pair with the rum, but other South Americans have worked for me also.

LIQUOR Ron Zacapa's rich, complex flavours stand tall paired with these other ingredients to create a lush full-flavoured spiciness.

6 HOMEMADE COFFEE PRODUCTS

On my journey creating coffee cocktails, I've made a number of handy and delicious homemade coffee products that you may find useful when making some of the recipes in this book, or to help create recipes of your own. There are often multiple ways to go about creating a recipe, so I have sometimes given you different options – choose the method that best suits you. All will give you different, but still good-quality, results.

Bartender's tips

• Gather all the items you need together at your station before you begin so you're not going back and forth all over the bar or kitchen.

• Clean as you go to stay on top of the mess and to help you work more efficiently.

• Taste as you go, so you can adjust as needed.

• Document your results so it's easier to replicate or improve with future batches.

• Please be aware of food safety hazards, local liquor laws, hazardous or restricted ingredients, and dangerous equipment.

COFFEE SYRUP
SIMPLE COLD BREW METHOD

The making of flavoured syrups is a fairly simple and popular way for bartenders to bring a touch of their own personal style and creativity to their drinks. A good coffee syrup has many uses – first of all, the sugar creates a more shelf-stable environment for the coffee, extending the shelf life and preserving the flavours of freshly extracted coffee by slowing oxidation. Secondly, it helps to boost coffee flavour, balance acidity and bitterness in cocktails and mocktails, as well as being a delicious addition to cream or doughnuts, cakes and desserts, etc. From simple grenadine recipes to complex orgeat varieties, there are numerous ways to go about making syrups. They can be boosted further by adding your favourite spices, such as cinnamon, vanilla bean, nutmeg, ginger, cloves, allspice and cacao nibs, to various parts of the process to add complexity. Below and opposite are the methods that I've found work extremely well. Choose the one that suits your needs or use them as inspiration to create your own.

250 ml/8½ oz cold brew coffee concentrate (using Toddy system: 250 g/9 oz coffee, 1 litre/33 oz water, 18 hrs)

500 ml/17 oz simple sugar syrup (2 parts sugar to 1 part water) (see page 55)

Pinch of salt

Combine the ingredients at room temperature in a large, clean mixing bowl and stir well until fully combined. Taste and adjust with more coffee or sugar to suit your personal balance preference. Funnel into a sterilized bottle and refrigerate for up to 4 weeks.

Spice this syrup by simply dropping the spices of your choice into the mixing bowl with the coffee and sugar syrup and allowing them time to infuse through cold maceration. You could use a single spice, such as cinnamon, or a blend of spices. Taste regularly and strain them out using a fine-mesh superbag (see page 42), once it reaches your desired flavour.

Note: certain spices such as cinnamon and cloves are stronger than others and will impart flavour a lot quicker, so always start small and build your way up. The salt is important as it softens, sweetens and amplifies the flavour.

COFFEE SYRUP
STOVETOP HOT BREW METHOD

This method is a little more traditional and technical but works just as well, if not better, to create a long-lasting and delicious coffee syrup.

150 g/5⅓ oz coarsely ground
  coffee of your choice
700 ml/23½ oz water
1 kg/5 cups caster/superfine sugar
Pinch of salt

Combine the coffee and water in a saucepan and slowly heat to simmer for approximately 3 minutes. Strain through a fine sieve/strainer then add the sugar and salt, return to the heat and gently bring to a simmer while stirring until the sugar is dissolved. Don't allow it to boil heavily.

Taste to ensure it has the correct coffee concentration of flavour, then remove from the heat and strain through a superbag (see page 42) or muslin cloth and allow to cool.

Funnel into a sterilized bottle and refrigerate for up to 6 weeks.

Note: this recipe is also simple to spice up by adding your preferred spices into the saucepan with the coffee and allowing the heat to extract the flavour, before straining with the coffee.

COFFEE LIQUEUR
COLD BREW BLEND METHOD

A natural progression from making syrups is to move on to homemade liqueurs. The addition of alcohol elevates and preserves the flavour of the syrup, as well as extending shelf life and softening sweetness. It is also a great way to extract the flavours from coffee, depending on the method used. The method below is a simple adjustment to the cold brew syrup method on page 184.

250 ml/8½ oz cold brew coffee concentrate (using Toddy system: 250 g/9 oz coffee, 1 litre/33 oz water, 18 hrs)

250 ml/8½ oz simple sugar syrup (3 parts sugar to 1 part water) (see page 55)

300 ml/10 oz spirit of your choice

Pinch of salt

Combine the ingredients at room temperature in a clean mixing bowl and stir well until fully combined. Taste and adjust with more coffee, sugar or spirit to suit your personal balance preference. Funnel into a sterilized bottle and refrigerate for up to 6 months.

LIQUOR While a high-proof liquor like Everclear would be ideal to use here, it isn't readily available in many countries. I have found a good-quality vodka works just fine, but why stop there? I've had even better results by using other spirits as the base. Rye whiskey, Bourbon, aged rum, Reposado tequila, brandy and many Scotch, Canadian and Irish whiskies can work really well – they each bring their own unique personalities to the party.

Note: Just like the syrups, these are easy to spice up. Simply add the spices of your choice into the mixing glass with the coffee, sugar syrup and spirit and allow them time to infuse through cold maceration. Taste regularly and strain them out once it reaches your desired flavour. Alternatively, place all the ingredients in a sealable vacuum bag and sous-vide (see page 205) for approximately 3 hours at 50°C/122°F.

COFFEE LIQUEUR
MACERATION METHOD

With this method it takes 12 hours to infuse the coffee into the spirit, and then it gets rounded out with the sugar.

150 g/5⅓ oz coarsely ground blended espresso roast coffee
700 ml/23½ oz spirit of your choice
500 g/2½ cups caster/superfine sugar
Pinch of salt

Combine the coffee and spirit in a large jar or French Press/cafetière. Allow to infuse for 12 hours, then strain through a superbag (see page 42) or muslin cloth.

Add sugar, stir periodically and wait for the sugar to dissolve completely. Taste to ensure the correct sweetness has been achieved and adjust to your preference. Funnel into a sterilized bottle and refrigerate for up to 8 months.

Rather than using the cold maceration technique, this process can be sped up by placing all the ingredients in a sealable vacuum bag and placing it in a sous-vide for approximately 3 hours at 50°C/122°F, followed by straining as per the above instructions.

Note: This recipe is also simple to spice up by adding your preferred spices, such as cinnamon, vanilla bean, nutmeg, ginger, cacao nibs, into the initial coffee and spirit infusion.

COFFEE ICE

The formulation of this all depends on the strength you prefer; adjust as necessary to suit your taste. Any monkey can put coffee in the freezer to make ice cubes, but below are a few tips I've learned from multiple attempts.

500 ml/17 oz cold brew coffee of
   your choice (see page 184)
300 ml/10 oz mineral water

Mix the ingredients together in a sterilized container and taste to test the strength. Once appropriate dilution is found, simply place in the freezer.

Freezer tips
• Other desired flavours can be added to your ice, such as vanilla extract, various spices and bitters.

• Ice that is made in a freezer containing food is easily tainted with foreign aromas, so the ideal scenario is that your freezer will only be used for ice, glassware and spirits.

• As well as standard ice-cube trays, experiment with other containers to produce different shapes and sizes of ice.

COFFEE SODA

Once you've made the coffee syrup, it's very simple to use as the base for your soda. Naturally this can also be a spiced coffee syrup, as per the requirement for the Cafe Corona recipe on page 139.

150 ml/5 oz homemade coffee syrup

550 ml/18¾ oz chilled mineral water (chilled water will carbonate faster)

0.01 g malic acid (citric or tartaric acids can also work)

Add all the ingredients to a 1 litre/33 oz soda syphon and charge with a CO_2 canister. Chill and allow to settle, ideally for 30 minutes before use.

Re-charge with gas as needed.

Note: Add the malic acid tentatively. Acid adds mouthfeel as well as stabilizing and extending shelf life.

BARREL-AGED COFFEE LIQUEUR

For barrel-aged coffee liqueur, simply add one of the previous liqueur recipes to an oak bottle or barrel and allow to rest in a cool place.

Bartender's notes and tips

• As with any maturation in oak, you are essentially adding another flavour to your product. Too little and it won't be noticed, too much and the oak can overpower the other ingredients. So taste it regularly to find that sweet spot. If you go too far, simply dilute by adding more of the original un-aged product.

• With ageing, the alcohol will evaporate so the strength will drop, causing the sugar concentration to rise and making a sweeter liquor.

• The fresher the barrel or bottle, the faster it will pass on its flavours.

• Using older, previously used barrels will affect your results. Liquors will age more slowly due to flavours having previously been extracted from the earlier batches. Also the flavour of the previous batches can pass into your current batch. This is called pre-seasoning. It can help or hinder your liqueur, depending on the previous contents. For example, a barrel that has previously held a Sweet Manhattan will pass on rye and rosso vermouth notes, whereas a previous batch of Negroni may pass on flavours you don't want in your liqueur.

• Likewise, after ageing your coffee liqueur, by using the vessel to age something else, it will take on the character of coffee – which could be a great addition to another cocktail.

FIG & HAZELNUT COLD BREW

This method works to add a subtle character of toasted nuts and the richness of dried figs to your cold brew. It's perhaps a little controversial to coffee geek purists, as it's tampering with the purity of quality coffee. However, I personally believe these types of infusions will be popular for baristas in the years to come as they look to explore new flavour combinations. I'm currently experimenting with ingredients such as apricots, cacao, Brazil nuts, almonds, cashews and hibiscus flowers, to see what they can offer. The idea is to subtly add to the coffee with natural flavours, being careful not to overpower or taint the coffee.

1,250 ml/42¼ oz mineral water
200 g/7 oz coarsely ground coffee
150 g/5⅓ oz finely chopped dried figs
100 g/3½ oz toasted coarsely ground hazelnuts

Mix the dry ingredients together, then proceed to make a batch of cold brew coffee as normal by adding the water and covering with a cloth.

Store in a cool, dry, dark space for 18 hours. Strain through a superbag, muslin cloth or Toddy filter (see page 41). Once strained, be sure to keep refrigerated.

COFFEE BITTERS

Aromatic cocktail bitters are essentially made by infusing botanicals, herbs, roots, flowers and spices in an alcohol solution that strips out the oils, acids, tannins, flavours and aromas to create a bitter alcohol extract. These days we are incredibly spoilt for choice with a huge array of products available on the market, which are produced by passionate people who have invested a lot of care, time and money into creating exceptional products so we don't have to. However, in saying that, I haven't come across too many coffee bitter options. In fact, we have zero available in Dubai, which drove me to experiment with making my own. Coffee has bitter and acidic components that will be infused rapidly into alcohol, but not always in a good way, as I discovered from the huge fails I suffered before I settled on the formula here. The touch of vanilla helps to round out the coffee and add a pleasant aroma, while the gentian root (most famously used in Angostura Bitters) adds complexity and a penetrative bitterness to the coffee that will help it to stand up more in cocktails.

30 g/1 oz dried vanilla bean

750 ml/25 oz Ketel One vodka

250 ml/8½ oz Bulleit Bourbon

250 g/9 oz medium ground (Chemex) coffee

1.5 g dried gentian root, coarsely ground

100 ml/3¼ oz Smirnoff Blue Label vodka (50% abv)

Split the vanilla pod and dice or grind into very small pieces and add to a large sterilized glass jar with the Ketel One, Bulleit Bourbon and coffee. Stir lightly and cover with a tea towel/dish towel – this is essential to protect it from light and to allow the CO_2 to escape.

In a separate jar, mix the gentian root and Smirnoff vodka, then seal. Store both items in a cool, dry, dark space.

Strain the coffee after 48 hours and the gentian tincture after 96 hours through a super-fine cloth filter and then through a well-rinsed paper filter to remove as much sediment as possible. Taste both and then slowly add in the gentian in small amounts and taste regularly until you find the balance you prefer. I tend to use 80–90 ml/2¾–3 oz, depending on the coffee used.

Note: Other spices, such as cacao nibs and cinnamon, can be added to these infusions to boost the bitterness and add further complex flavours. The recommended method is to infuse spices into spirits separately and then blend with the finished infusions to achieve accurate and consistent flavour balance.

COFFEE A medium roast honey processed single origin Arabica works well for this method. I use a bean I'm familiar with using for cold brew. A rich Colombian or Guatemalan with cacao and caramel character is ideal.

LIQUOR Liquor strength will make a huge impact on the flavour extraction. High-proof liquor is ideal but can be tough to acquire, so quality vodka is a good alternative. Other spirits can work too, but their big flavours can overpower your chosen ingredients, which is why I use a blend for this recipe. If you want to get really crazy, you can blend in a small amounts of other spirits such as mezcal or peated whisky to add smokiness. However, these experiments can be costly and won't always work.

COFFEE-INFUSED VERMOUTH

This adds a deep coffee note to a sweet vermouth and is a method I use frequently for adding subtle coffee character to stirred cocktails. The intensity level can be controlled by the ratio of ground coffee added to the vermouth.

700 ml/23½ oz rosso (sweet) vermouth

100 g/3½ oz coarsely ground coffee

Mix the ingredients together in a sterilized container and cover with a cotton cloth. Store in a cool, dry, dark space for 2–6 hours.

Strain through a Toddy filter (see page 41) or fine mesh superbag (see page 42), bottle and then keep refrigerated.

COFFEE Pair the vermouth with a single origin roast with characters that will complement it.

LIQUOR As vermouths can vary vastly from brand to brand, I suggest tasting your vermouth and then selecting a coffee to match it. Perhaps even take a sample of vermouth to your roaster to taste and he or she can help you decide. By adding a touch of cold brew into the vermouth, you'll get a good example of the finished result.

COFFEE-INFUSED SPIRIT
IMMERSION METHOD

Like the vermouth recipe opposite, the formulation of this all depends on the strength you prefer. I always look to create a harmonious balance between the coffee and spirit. Ideally I want the spirit to shine through and the coffee to play a supporting role to accent the drink. As with other infusions, always select a quality coffee roast that will complement your spirit.

700 ml/23½ oz spirit of your choice
80 g/2¾ oz coarsely ground coffee

Mix the ingredients together in a sterilized container and cover with a cloth. Store in a cool, dark space for 16 hours.

Strain through a superbag (see page 42), muslin cloth or Toddy filter (see page 41).

Note: I have tried to filter infusions through paper many times, but I feel that the paper strips out the character from the spirits, leaving them drier and spicier than I like. If you need to use paper, then make sure you first run 1–2 litres/33–66 oz of water through it – this will open up the microns (pores) to allow a better flow with less impact on the spirit.

NITRO-INFUSED COFFEE SPIRIT NITRO-CAVITATION METHOD

The formulation of this all depends on the strength you prefer. I like to add it as a subtle flavour that blends in well with the coffee, but you can up the ratio to lift the coffee flavour if that's your preference . Other desired flavours can easily be added to the infusion, such as vanilla bean, nutmeg and dried orange.

600 ml/20 oz spirit of your choice
150 g/5⅓ oz coarsely ground
   coffee

Mix the spirit and coffee together in a thoroughly cleaned cream syphon. Seal and shake, then charge with two canisters of NO_2 gas. Shake, allow to settle for 3 minutes then release the gas and strain through a superbag, muslin cloth or Toddy filter (see page 41). Bottle the infused spirit.

TIRAMISU ICE CREAM

I must admit I can't resist the allure of a good Tiramisu after dinner (in fact, my wife calls it my kryptonite). So a homemade Tiramisu ice cream I could use for cocktails was a fun experiment I had to do – and the results are sensational. For this recipe I've listed two methods. Both use fairly expensive pieces of equipment to achieve nice smooth textures – if you don't have access to these, simply blend the mixture hard and fast to fill it full of air and then freeze it and scoop as needed.

200 ml/6¾ oz cold brew coffee
200 g/7 oz mascarpone
300 ml/10 oz full-fat/heavy cream
1 egg yolk
120 ml/4 oz VS Cognac
45 ml/1½ oz honey
45 ml/1½ oz dark Crème de Cacao

Combine the ingredients in a blender and mix well.

Method 1: Add to an ice-cream machine and churn/freeze until thick and smooth.

Method 2: Freeze solid in a Paco jet canister, fit this to the machine and blend it in layers under the vacuum as needed.

COFFEE FOAM

Foams became a special ingredient for bartenders to use from around 2006 and have ridden waves of popularity in different countries ever since. It was a method borrowed from chefs as bartenders began to get curious about the innovative dishes coming out of the kitchen. There are numerous ways to make airs and foams. They require an emulsifying agent such as egg white, lecithin or sucrose paired with a flavouring agent and often sugar. The recipe below is for a very simple smooth foam that will hold up well when layered on top of cocktails, without being gloopy.

150 ml/5 oz pasteurized egg white

150 ml/5 oz full-strength cold brew coffee of your choice

150 ml/5 oz sugar syrup (see page 55)

2.2 g Sucro (see opposite page)

1.2 g Xantana (see opposite page)

Mix the ingredients together in a sterilized container with a stick blender to combine well. Pour into an iSi cream whipping syphon and charge with 2x NO_2 cartridges (not CO_2).

Keep refrigerated and use as needed. Approximate shelf life is 2 weeks.

COFFEE AIR

Airs are lighter and fluffier than foams and have bigger bubbles – think of bubble bath foam rather than cappuccino foam. There are numerous ways to make them using the emulsifying agents lecithin or sucrose paired with a flavouring agent. I prefer to use Sucro and Xantana, products from the Texturas range, which will help to create hold and volume – they are more stable than lecithin. The recipe below is for a very simple smooth air that will hold up well when layered on top of cocktails.

150 ml/5 oz full-strength cold brew coffee of your choice
6 g Sucro
0.2 g Xantana

Mix the ingedients together in a sterilized container with a stick blender or electric whisk to combine well. Pour into a wide-mouth container and add a hose from a fish tank oxygenator (available from most pet stores). Switch it on and watch the bubbles rise.

Scoop the bubbles on to your drink and turn off the oxygen until you need it for the next drink. I tend to make this mixture daily as needed and then discard after use.

CHOCOLATE COFFEE GANACHE

Smooth, rich, velvety chocolate ganache is basically liquid heaven! To make it you simply add hot cream and butter to your favourite chocolate. Naturally the addition of coffee and liquor enhances it to even greater heights. When made well, you can store it in the refrigerator for months and it will remain as a smooth liquid chocolate you can drink on its own, use to rim glasses (pictures opposite, bottom left and right) or add to cocktails and desserts.

300 g/10 oz dark chocolate (approx 60 per cent cacao), cut into small pieces
400 ml/13½ oz whipping cream
25 g/¼ stick unsalted butter
105 ml/3½ oz cold brew coffee
2 ml Madagascar vanilla extract
Pinch of salt
105 ml/3½ oz Bourbon

Bring 300 ml/10 oz water to a simmer in a saucepan.

Place the chocolate in a medium-sized heatproof bowl and set to the side.

Put the cream, butter, coffee and vanilla extract into a separate pan and stir over a medium heat until the mixture begins to simmer (picture top right).

Place the chocolate bowl over the simmering water in the pan. Pour the cream and butter mixture over the chocolate and fold together to mix (picture middle left).

Slowly add in the bourbon while whisking hard to bind everything together. If it starts to split, add more cream and continue to whisk until it becomes velvety smooth. It should stick to the back of a spoon but drizzle off fluidly (picture middle right). Season with salt to taste.

Remove from the heat, allow to cool and put into a sterilized squeezy bottle. Refrigerate.

COFFEE EAU DE VIE AROMA

The Rotary Evaporator is essentially a science lab grade still that performs distillation under vacuum pressure. This means it can extract essences without using high temperatures which change flavours, giving bartenders the opportunity to experiment and create interesting ingredients to use for cocktails. I've personally made some great extracts such as pineapple gin, caramelized banana, leather, peanut butter and freshly cut grass. The following instructions explain a fairly simple way to create a clean, clear coffee aroma that can be added into drinks or sprayed over the top.

500 ml/17 oz cold brew coffee vodka (strong immersion cold brew coffee made with vodka rather than water at a 5:1 ratio)

Check the Rotavap to ensure it's clean, valves are sealed, the receiving flask is secure and everything is ready to go. Turn it on and set the cooling condenser temperature to -12°C/10°F. Fill the water bath with room temperature water and set the temperature to 30°C/86°F.

When both the water and condenser temperatures reach your settings, add the coffee vodka to the evaporator flask, attach securely and lower it into the water.

Turn on the external vacuum pump. Set the rotation to 150 and begin the rotation. Note: the faster it spins, the higher/faster the distillation rate. To achieve the best results I recommend monitoring it closely for the first 10–15 minutes to ensure the flask rotation speed and the bath temperatures are set correctly. Adjust these as needed to extract efficiently, being careful not to boil over. These can generally both be lifted as the distillation progresses.

If you can smell your distillate, you are likely losing quality compounds which means your condenser isn't cool enough or a valve is open. If the mixture starts to bubble, it can boil over and spoil your distillate. To counter this, lower the water bath temperature and slow down the rotation speed to find a sweet spot that is stable but is still distilling fast enough.

It's complete once the sediment in the evaporation flask becomes a thickish, gloopy paste.

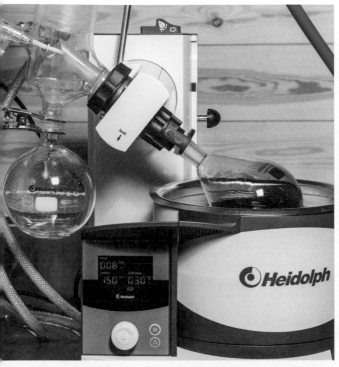

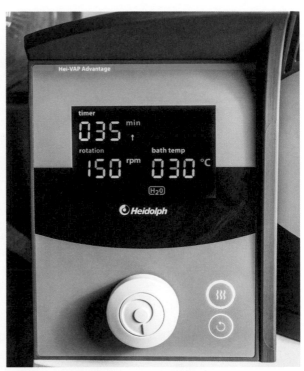

GLOSSARY

Aeration When air is added into a liquid.

Amarena Small, dark, sour Italian cherries preserved in a rich sugar syrup.

Amaro Italian word for bitter, often referring to a bitter herbal liqueur.

Arabica An evergreen species of coffee plant regarded to produce better coffee than other species – 100% Arabica is preferred.

Atomizer A small bottle to spray aromatics on to drinks.

Barista A person that specializes in brewing coffee for a living.

Bitters An aromatic cocktail ingredient that can be made from roots, flowers, fruits, spices and/or herbs, which have been infused into a base of alcohol to balance and add complex flavours.

Blazer A spirit-based drink which is ignited on fire and passed between two vessels to heat, blend and dissolve sugars.

Bloom The technique of saturating freshly ground coffee with a small amount of water and then resting it for a short time to allow the CO_2 to escape the coffee, to minimize carbonic acid.

Brew ratio The ratio of water to coffee used to extract the flavours – for example, 5:1 = 5 parts water to 1 part coffee.

Cafetière A French Press or plunger.

Chemex An hourglass-shaped vessel designed to brew pour-over coffee using a paper filter.

Chinese 5 spice A mix of spices used mostly for Chinese cooking. A blend of cinnamon, star anise, cloves, fennel seeds and Szechuan peppercorns. Some recipes also contain nutmeg, ginger and licorice.

Cold brew Coffee brewed at room temperature using longer contact time rather than heat to extract its flavours.

Cold drip Coffee extracted using a dripping process, using time and gravity to extract the flavours.

Coupette Also referred to as a champagne coupe, it's a stemmed glass similar to a classic Martini glass but with a rounded rather than V shape.

Cream syphon Often called an iSi gun, this is a canister designed to be charged with NO_2 or CO_2 gas to carbonate or foam ingredients such as cream or egg white for culinary foams.

Crema The aerated foam floating on the surface of coffee, particularly espresso.

Cultivar A coffee variety which has been cultivated for commercial purposes.

Dallah An Arabic coffee pot used to brew and serve Arabic coffee called Qahwa.

Dark roast Coffee, which is often oily, roasted to a dark chocolate colour.

Dash A very small unit of measurement equal to approximately one millilitre.

Double strain Using hawthorn and mesh basket strainers to remove fine particles when straining from a shaker into a glass.

Dry process *See* "Natural process", opposite.

Eau de vie A clear fruit distillate.

Flaming zest The process of igniting the oils in orange or lemon zest to create a caramelized aroma over the surface of a drink.

Ganache Liquid chocolate.

Golden syrup A traditional English caramelized liquid sugar used for baking.

Half & half A blend of half cream and half milk.

Honey process A coffee-harvesting method where the outer skin is removed and then the beans are left to dry with the mucilage (pulp) intact.

Ibrik A long-handled Turkish coffee pot.

Light roast Lightly roasted coffee.

Malic acid A type of natural fruit acid, often associated with apples.

Mocha/Moka/Mokha Mocha is a cappuccino/hot chocolate hybrid. A Moka pot is an Italian stovetop brewer. Mokha is a port in Yemen where coffee's journey to the rest of the world began.

Mouthfeel The textures, temperatures and overall touch sensations felt in the mouth when tasting food and drink.

Mucilage The fruit pulp/flesh that lies under the coffee cherries' skin and sticks to the coffee seeds.

Natural process Naturally drying the coffee cherries in the sun after harvest, before removing the inner seeds.

Nitro-cavitation The process of rapidly infusing flavours into liquids using nitrogen gas in a cream syphon.

Pacojet A powerful blender that works under vacuum pressure to micro-blend and aerate frozen ingredients – it is ideal for ice cream and sorbet.

Pimento Dram A rum and pimento (allspice) liqueur.

Portafilter The handle and basket head used to brew coffee for espresso.

Pour-over Coffee-brewing method of pouring water into coffee grinds over a filter.

Pre-batched To pre-mix ingredients together in advance of service to aid speed and consistency.

Robusta A robust species of coffee tree that produces coffee with low acidity and high bitterness – primarily used for instant coffee.

SCA Specialty Coffee Association, a representative group for high-quality coffee.

Single origin Coffee grown within a single known geographic origin to showcase particular traits.

Sous-vide A temperature-controlled water bath used for cooking and infusing flavours.

Speciality coffee Coffee beans of the best quality and flavour that are produced in special micro-climates.

Speculaas A spiced biscuit popular in Holland, Belgium and Germany.

Sucro An emulsifier powder from the Texturas range, which is ideal for aerating liquids for foams and airs.

Sugar syrup Cane sugar dissolved into water in equal parts (1:1 ratio), unless otherwise stated. A 2:1 ratio is often popular also.

Superbag A nylon mesh bag used for filtering/straining out fine particles from liquids.

Swizzle To mix cocktail ingredients by vigorously spinning a barspoon or swizzle stick

Tamp A weighted flat stamp for evenly pressing coffee into the portafilter for espresso.

Terroir The environmental character passed on to coffee/wine etc, which can be detected through tasting.

Throw To toss a cocktail between two shakers to mix, chill, dilute and aerate it.

Toddy System A brand name for a set of equipment designed for immersion cold brew production.

V60 A tool used to hold a paper filter used for pour-over coffee. Created by Japanese company Harrio, the name comes from the 60 degree angle of the sides.

Vermouth Wine, originating from the mid-1700s in Turin, Italy, aromatized with botanicals and fortified with spirits. It should be stored in the fridge.

Washed process A method of removing the skin and pulp from the coffee cherry using large amounts of water.

Xantana A xanthum gum powder, made by the Texturas range, used to thicken liquids.

INDEX

ABOUT THE AUTHOR

Living in New Zealand, quality coffee culture and appreciation was all around me from a young age, so it was only natural that the tasks of drawing a flawless espresso, frothing perfect milk and pouring that perfect flat white became challenges that the competitive O.C.D. flavour fiend in me just had to embrace.

Mixing the coffee with liquor just seemed natural to me and over the years I've enjoyed surprising people with just how versatile the two can be together, which I guess is what led me to write this book.

I can still recall my first ever experience of drinking coffee and liquor together. In 1997, I was a baby-faced 17-year-old working as a glass collector in a party bar. Midway through an excruciatingly busy shift, cleaning up after a stampede of thirsty punters, my bar captain slipped out the back with two shot glasses full of three carefully layered liquids he'd confiscated from what could politely be called an overly excited guest. I necked it and...wow! What a pleasant surprise that ensued. The top layer of sweet orange was still warm from the flame he had recently extinguished, followed by a caramel creaminess, then the sweet but unmistakable kick of coffee. My B52 cherry had been popped! With a big grin on my face and

a spring in my step, I went back to collecting dirty glasses at record speeds.

In the years that followed, I learnt to pour them for myself, along with both Black and White Russians, Irish Coffees, the Colorado Bulldog, FBI and of course the infamous Espresso Martini. After a stint as a barista in 2002, I began to combine my experience from both trades towards developing my own coffee and liquor cocktail recipes.

I recently celebrated 20 years of working in the bar industry, having worked my way up through a wide variety of roles across various venues in four different countries.

I have proudly represented the New Zealand bar community in multiple global cocktail competitions over the years, including the 42 Below Cocktail World Cup, IBA World Final, Bols Around the World, and the Appleton Estate World Final. The highlight, though, was competing in the Diageo World Class Global finals in 2013 and 2014, where I finished 4th overall in 2013.

These events have given me a passion to share my experience and knowledge with other bartenders to help them follow their dreams.

ACKNOWLEDGEMENTS

I'd like to clink glasses with and offer high-fives to the team of people that has helped me to bring this project to life...

My wife **Venetia Tiarks-Clark** for her constant support and encouragement through thick and thin.

My phenomenal photographer **Alex Attitov Osyka** and his assistant: www.alexattitov.com.

My father, **Graham Clark,** for his guidance and support.

Daniel Jon Miles for his writing expertise, time, advice and encouragement, which really helped me package a polished product.

Dubai Coffee Museum: Supplier of the timeline (pp.16–19): www.coffeemuseum.ae. A brilliant exhibition of the Middle East's rich coffee history and industry.

My employer **African + Eastern**, the best liquor distributor in the Middle East/world!

My old buddy **Ben Jones** for his design wisdom and positive energy.

Muddle Me Bar Supplies, Dubai, for their support with stunning glassware and tools: www.muddle-me.com.

Night Jar Coffee Roasters: www.nightjar.coffee.

T&J Catering, Dubai, for sharing some stunning glassware: www.tjdubai.com.

Classic fine foods: www.classicfinefoods.com.

Acen Razvi for his amazing videography support: www.acenrasvi.com.

To the many brands that offered support, which I didn't take (yet), because I preferred this to be open-minded, using the brands I like and am familiar with.

Chef Jean-Francoise of Cafe Choix Patisserie and Classic Fine Foods, Dubai, for putting together my chocolate spheres for my favourite cocktail in this book.

My publisher for taking a gamble on me and pushing the boundaries to get it released quickly.

And... to every passionate bartender and barista I have met along my journey!

Thank you for taking the time to read my book and I hope you find some inspiration within to help you make more people enjoy the art and craft of coffee cocktails!

Cheers to you all,

JC